1.00
K

INTERNATIONAL CHRISTIAN
GRADUATE UNIVERSITY

D1064657

CURRENT PROBLEMS

General Editor:

Sir Ernest Barker, Litt.D.

PACIFISM AND
CONSCIENTIOUS OBJECTION

24

CURRENT PROBLEMS

General Editor: SIR ERNEST BARKER

PACIFISM AND CONSCIENTIOUS OBJECTION

BY

G. C. FIELD, M.A., D.Litt.

*Professor of Philosophy in the
University of Bristol*

CAMBRIDGE

AT THE UNIVERSITY PRESS

1945

CAMBRIDGE
UNIVERSITY PRESS

LONDON: BENTLEY HOUSE

NEW YORK, TORONTO, BOMBAY
CALCUTTA, MADRAS: MACMILLAN

All rights reserved

PRINTED IN GREAT BRITAIN

INTERNATIONAL CHRISTIAN
GRADUATE UNIVERSITY

CONTENTS

JX
1952
F 454
1945

22676

PREFACE

This study is based, in the first place, on the statements made by the several thousands of conscientious objectors who have appeared before the Tribunal of which I was a member from the middle of 1940 until my resignation at the end of 1944. These statements, like all the proceedings of the Tribunals, were public and have been, on occasions, reproduced in the Press. I have not, of course, made use of any material which was not public property. In addition, I have used some of the more systematic expositions of Pacifism, of which I would single out as specially worthy of attention the book by Dr Cadoux referred to in the text. I am indebted to Dr Cadoux for further elucidation of some of the points raised in this work in the course of a correspondence exchanged between us. But it has seemed to me that what particularly calls for examination is the type of argument which appeals to those who have actually had to take the practical decision of objecting to military service.

These arguments were to be found in the first place in the written statements that every applicant was invited to submit to the Tribunal. These varied in length, to take the extreme cases in our own experience, from an essay thirty pages long to a one-line statement, 'I do not believe in war'. The average was much nearer the latter than the former. The applicant was then given the opportunity to enlarge on this statement and could be questioned on it by the Tribunal. It was, of course, no part of the functions of the Tribunal to argue the merits of the case, though it must be confessed that in some cases the interest of the discussion may have led us to carry it on beyond what was strictly necessary to establish the genuineness of the application. But it was often necessary for the Tribunal to satisfy itself that the applicant had given sufficient serious consideration to the question to warrant his application being regarded as a genuine conscientious objection. And it was also often necessary to get clear about the precise grounds of the objection in order to see how far it could be regarded as applying to one or other of the alternative forms of service open to the conscientious objector. This was a point to which even some of the most serious objectors often seemed to have given very inadequate consideration, and it was the point which in our experience occupied by far the greater part of the time and attention of the Tribunal. There was, therefore, the widest opportunity for members of the Tribunal to acquaint themselves with the arguments and considerations which had the greatest influence on the practical decisions of conscientious objectors.

I should like to acknowledge my indebtedness for many illuminating discussions to my fellow-members of the South-Western Tribunal, above all to our chairman, Judge E. H. C. Wethered. But what follows is purely an expression of my own individual views, and must not be regarded as in any way committing any other member, still less, of course, the Tribunal as a body.

Certain passages in this work have already appeared in print in a paper contributed by me to the *Proceedings of the Aristotelian Society*.

G. C. FIELD

1944

CHAPTER I

INTRODUCTION

The two great wars of the present century have brought the question of the morality of participation in war as an immediate practical problem to the minds of many people. But the issue is not, of course, a new one: indeed, the debate goes back for many centuries. In ancient societies, particularly those in which some form of free institutions had developed, it was taken for granted that membership of the society involved the duty of taking up arms for it when necessary. The first clear challenge to this assumption came from early Christianity. It cannot be claimed that the Christian body was ever unanimously pacifist. From its very early days there seem to have been Christians serving in the Roman armies. But undoubtedly the predominant view of the leading thinkers and teachers in the Christian Church in the first two centuries of its existence was that the Christian should not participate in warfare. It must be recognised, however, that in most cases this was part of a wider repudiation of the duty of a Christian to take any part in the public service of a non-Christian state. The *militiae*, which the Christian Fathers rejected, included service in a civilian as much as in a military capacity. The Christian's kingdom was not of this world, and he felt little obligation to the pagan kingdoms of this world except to work for their conversion.

It was natural, therefore, that when the Roman Empire became officially Christian the attitude of the Christian Church towards service on behalf of it should change, particularly when it was a question of defending a Christian society against the attacks of non-Christian or even of unorthodox Christian enemies. From the time of Constantine to the Reformation uncompromising Pacifism practically disappears from Christian thought. Yet certain concessions to it were made in the ideas developed through that long period. In the first place, the doctrine of vocation regarded the religious life, the highest form of life open to men, as incompatible with active participation in warfare. Secondly, the Schoolmen of the thirteenth century developed the theory of the 'just war' in which alone a Christian could legitimately take part, thus recognising the possibility of circumstances in which it might be the duty of a Christian to refuse the commands of his superior to fight. It is interesting to note that the small body of Pacifists in the Roman Catholic Church at the present time generally base their Pacifism on this doctrine. It is not open to them, in view of the previous teaching of the Church, to deny the theoretical possibility that it might be a duty to fight in some kinds of war. But they argue that the nature of modern warfare is such that in practice the conditions laid down for a just war cannot be fulfilled.

The ferment of new ideas which characterised the period of the Reformation produced a revival of pacifist theories, and certain religious bodies, for instance some groups of Anabaptists and later the

Quakers, adopted a completely pacifist doctrine. But their influence was very limited, and a more powerful stimulus probably came from the liberal, humanitarian movements of the eighteenth and nineteenth centuries, which were independent of, though sometimes allied with, particular religious beliefs. Movements of this kind took the standpoint of human welfare on this earth, and from that standpoint attacked the idea of the inevitability, and even more uncompromisingly the desirability, of war as an institution. Dislike of war is, of course, very far from being identical with Pacifism, but the passage from one to the other was easy for those who regarded war as the chief evil from which humanity had to be saved.

Modern Pacifism, therefore, has a mixed pedigree, and it is not surprising that it takes a variety of different forms. This great divergence between the positions taken up by different conscientious objectors is the first thing that experience on a Conscientious Objectors' Tribunal teaches one. On the Tribunal of which I was a member we listed adherents of fifty-one different religious bodies. And, though these did not all differ sharply from one another in the grounds of their Pacifism, a considerable number did. In addition there were those, comparatively few in number, whose objections were based on ethical or humanitarian grounds independently of any religious beliefs. And there were a few whom we classified as political objectors, and a few, also, who could only be described as objectors on aesthetic grounds. All these agreed in the one practical conclusion of refusing to participate in actual fighting. But the further conclusions that they drew often differed as widely as the premises from which they drew them.

It will be seen, then, that Pacifism or Conscientious Objection is not one single simple creed, but a number of creeds, based on widely different and sometimes diametrically opposed general principles. This obviously makes the task of critical evaluation particularly difficult. Indeed, it would not be too much to say that criticism of Pacifism is impossible: there can only be criticism of various pacifist arguments, some of which have little or no connection and may, indeed, be in contradiction with one another.

This raises a further difficulty. It is a cardinal principle of sound criticism that in discussing the truth or falsehood of any position the arguments for it should be taken at their strongest, and that we should not make too much play with the feebler arguments with which every position, right or wrong, has at times been supported. Yet it may equally be a matter of dispute among the advocates of a view, which are the strongest and most important arguments for it. To non-pacifists a book, for instance, such as Dr C. J. Cadoux's *Christian Pacifism Re-examined*, must seem one of the fairest, most reasonable and most persuasive of the presentations of the case for Pacifism. But there is no doubt that many Pacifists would not feel that he had penetrated to the core of their position, and some would probably feel that his fairness of mind had led him to make concessions to criticism which they would be unwilling to accept.

Apart from this it is desirable to point out, without dwelling on it unduly, how very far many pacifist arguments are from reaching the level of Dr Cadoux. Some, indeed, can only be dismissed as the product of ignorance or confusion of thought. We had applicants at the Tribunal who stated that they never knew that the Bible was not originally written in English. This was exceptional. But a much greater number showed an entire failure to realise that this fact was relevant to the interpretation of particular texts. Again, we became quite familiar with the assertion by members of certain religious bodies that if we would lay down our arms and trust in God, He would work a special miracle to save us. When the question has been asked whether they had any evidence that this sort of thing ever actually happened, we have received, not once but several times, the reply, 'Well, look at the miracle of Dunkirk!' 'The Prime Minister said it was a miracle', as one applicant added. Or again, we were confronted, time and again, with the confident historical generalisation that no war ever settled anything, only to find, on further inquiry, that the applicant knew nothing at all about any war except the last one. What is most remarkable about this is the apparent inability to realise that some knowledge of history is desirable as a basis for sweeping historical generalisations.

I do not mention these things to suggest that, in any sense, they prove Pacifism in all its forms to be wrong. But they do require to be mentioned, because of the tendency of some pacifist writers and speakers to claim a special degree of authority for the views of conscientious objectors on the ground of their alleged superiority in intelligence, courage, independence of mind and freedom from prejudice. 'As a rule it requires much more personal grit and character to be a C.O. than to become a soldier', wrote the *Bulletin of the Central Board for Conscientious Objectors* in October 1942. And in the same number we read that conscientious objectors 'are much better mentally equipped than the average individual: they must have cultivated the habit of study and have disciplined themselves in many ways before they could arrive at the fateful conclusion to resist the awful power of the State'.*

I venture to say that no one who has interviewed several thousand conscientious objectors at a Tribunal would endorse this estimate. The great majority of them fall into one or other of several well-defined classes. And the regularity with which the arguments, and even the phraseology, of the different groups are repeated by one applicant after another suggests much rather a ready-made set of ideas taken over from other people than an individual and independent examination of the problem. Statements which really reveal an original and independent approach are as rare as they are refreshing. The same conclusion emerges from the fact that the majority of the applicants who have been before us have been brought up in pacifist homes or with strong family or other influences in that

---

* It is worth pointing out that, as provision is made for conscientious objection by law, the great majority of them are never called upon to 'resist the awful power of the State'.

direction. It is fair to say that for a young man or woman with affectionate or dominating parents—we have seen plenty of both at the Tribunal—brought up in a religious sect that was either definitely pacifist or had a strong and well-organised pacifist movement within it, it would need considerably more strength and independence of mind to join the army than to be a conscientious objector. Similarly with the claim for freedom from emotional prejudice. It seems to be assumed in the arguments of many Pacifists that the passions and emotions aroused in war are the only source of prejudice worthy of serious consideration, and that, because they are free from the influence of war-like feelings, they are necessarily free from all prejudice and are, to a unique degree, capable of making dispassionate and impartial judgements. In reality, of course, any strong emotion, good or bad, can equally influence one's thinking. The passion for peace and the dread of war can certainly become very intense emotions, and, however amiable they may be, they are just as likely to distort and cloud the judgement as the war-like emotions of non-pacifists.

There is one special point that arises in this connection, though the development of it will carry us forward to certain general considerations which affect the whole discussion. Conscientious objectors are often asked such questions as 'Do you approve of a police force?' or 'Would you protect your mother by force if she were attacked by a murderous criminal?' And if their answer is in the affirmative they are often told that they have no right to object to war, 'because it is only a difference of degree'. Dr Cadoux, in the book referred to above, argues that a difference of degree may often make the difference between right and wrong or good and bad, and that there is nothing necessarily inconsistent in approving of a limited use of force, such as would be involved in the above cases, and disapproving of the much greater degree of force involved in a war.*

As a general principle, most of those who have given serious thought to ethical questions would have to agree that Dr Cadoux's argument is correct. Just as in the human body a small dose of strychnine will act as a tonic, while a large dose will be fatal, so in the body politic a limited amount of, let us say, restriction of individual liberty by the State is the condition of a good society, while an excessive amount is a positive evil. We should all recognise now the fallacy in the kind of argument which we used to hear in the days when one could still meet apologists for Nazism in this country. Anyone who objected to the complete suppression of all individual liberty in a totalitarian

---

* One ground of distinction, however, sometimes put forward by more thoughtful objectors, though plausible at first sight, appears unsound on further examination. It is urged that in keeping order within a community we are acting in obedience to an established and recognised law, under a recognised authority for enforcing it, whereas in war each power is fighting for itself at its own arbitrary will. This may be true at the present time. But it ignores the procedure by which in the past law and the lawful authority have come to be established and recognised. It is obvious that we could not get an established and recognised authority internationally without fighting, just as in the past it has often been necessary to fight to get one established within the State.

State could expect to be met by the retort, 'Well, you don't believe in allowing everyone to do exactly what they want. It's only a question of degree.' But obviously here the question of degree makes all the difference. Even the law, which is essentially a system of general rules, has to recognise this in some cases. Thus, to charge interest on a loan is recognised as just and proper. But if the interest extorted is too great it becomes 'harsh and unconscionable', and the law will protect the debtor. Yet this is a matter of degree, and no one could claim to fix, to a fraction of a penny, a precise point at which the amount became unjustifiable.

When this argument is used, however, as a general defence of Pacifists, there are two observations which require to be made.

In the first place, only a small minority of Pacifists, if the experience of our Tribunal is any guide, succeed in grasping this point for themselves. The great majority seem to demand an absolute rule of universal validity, admitting of no differences of degree, from which to deduce their objection to taking part in warfare. Most commonly they go for this rule to the supposed commandments of Scripture, though this is sometimes fortified by more general ethical arguments. We have sometimes been told that the text, 'Resist not evil', means that no Christian under any circumstances ought ever to use any kind of force. We have very often been presented with the argument that the Sixth Commandment means that in no possible circumstances is any taking of human life justifiable. It is in that connection, incidentally, that we most often found the entire inability to grasp the possibility that any question of the correct translation of the original text could arise. Equally surprising is the inability to see that the whole history recorded in the Old Testament makes it perfectly obvious that the Jews, among whom the commandment first arose, cannot possibly have understood it in this sense.* We have also become familiar with the argument that a man who takes life in peacetime is punished as a murderer—a statement, by the way, which is not invariably true—so that it is absurd to regard taking life as a duty in time of war. The implications of such an argument are clearly that, if taking life in any one set of circumstances is wrong, it must be equally wrong in all, however much they may differ. When they base their case on such supposed absolute, universal rules, without recognising the possibility of any degree in the extent of their applicability, it is the Pacifists who are committing the precise fallacy against which Dr Cadoux protests. And to such people the kind of question that he objects to is perfectly legitimate. For anyone who bases his case on a supposed universal law may fairly be asked to consider extreme cases to see if he has really understood the implications of the universal rule which he is putting forward.

The second observation follows from this. If we apply this principle of 'quantitative thinking', as

* Less educated Pacifists may be forgiven for making this error when we find it committed by a well-known writer in a letter to the *Spectator* some years ago.

Graham Wallas used to call it, and refuse to be guided rigidly by absolute general rules without regard to the special circumstances of particular cases, we must apply it consistently. And this is just what even so enlightened a pacifist writer as Dr Cadoux fails to do. He recognises different degrees of justifiability, according to the circumstances, in the use of force up to the point of war. And then he lays down an absolute general rule that no war is justified whatever the circumstances. Yet wars differ in their circumstances as widely as anything else. We do not wage 'war' in the abstract, but a particular war in particular conditions, and, above all, as an alternative to a particular set of evils which seem to us more evil than war. The evil of the possible alternatives to a war will obviously vary greatly in degree in each particular case. And it is hard to see how anyone who recognises the general validity of this method of thought can claim to be able to assert *a priori*, without considering the circumstances, that the evil of the possible alternatives can never be greater than the evil of war. It is the same with the wider generalisation that we must have heard repeated some hundreds of times that 'you cannot attain a good end by evil means'. This may, indeed, be merely a tautology hardly worth saying. But if what is meant is that a course of action, which we should not choose for its own sake or which has some evil features or evil accompaniments, cannot possibly in any circumstances produce in the final result a balance of good over evil, then it is plainly false.

When we come to the more specific arguments that

have been used to justify conscientious objections, there are some which will have to be dismissed with a word. Among these, there are in the first place what we have been accustomed to speak of as political objections. This class is not precisely definable, but by it I mean, in general, objections which are not properly pacifist, in the sense that they do not necessarily involve objection to participation in any kind of war, but which are based on supposed features in the political situation from which the present war arose. Such arguments are most often found associated with more strictly pacifist arguments. But not infrequently they have been put forward as the sole ground of objection.

How much weight, if any, should be attached to such objections? In some cases clearly very little. It would obviously be impossible rationally to defend the view that any disagreement on matters of policy with the established Government is sufficient ground for refusing obedience. Yet some of the objections that we have heard seem to come perilously near this position. The criticisms of British policy in the years before the war, when put forward as a ground for conscientious objection to military service now, would generally be of this type. We have even had applicants, such is the perversity of which the human mind is capable, who have objected to taking part in this war because Great Britain had not intervened earlier to check aggression by force. It would obviously be waste of time to discuss such views seriously. Hardly more serious are the arguments based on reflections on the character or motives of particular politicians. It would be fair to say that no position can be regarded as a matter of conscience if it is based on assertions of fact about matters on which it is impossible for the asserter to be adequately informed, like the young man who told us that all Members of Parliament, except Mr D. N. Pritt and Mr Gallacher, were dishonest. It is the same with assertions about the motives of various British statesmen put forward by people who had no personal knowledge of these statesmen and very scanty knowledge of recent political events.

A word may be said, because of the instructive fallacies that it enshrines, about one type of assertion that we have met on several occasions. That is the assertion, in one form or another, that Great Britain did not enter the war for the defence of Poland (or any other of the ostensible reasons) but for the protection of her own Imperialist interests, or some similar phrase. It is an interesting exercise to analyse the fallacies that this contains. Apart from the questions of fact involved, there are two general fallacies here of particular importance. The first is the fallacy, only too common in other connections, of talking of Great Britain as if 'she' were a single, individual person, and, what is more, unlike most real individual persons, only capable of being actuated by one single motive at a time. In reality, of course, the final operative decision was taken by the Cabinet, itself composed of a number of individuals who, in all probability, like most human beings, were affected by a number of different motives. Further, they could not possibly have come to this decision unless they had been supported, and indeed urged on by countless other individuals, probably the great majority of the nation. The responsibility for the final decision belongs, in varying degrees, to all these individuals, among whom all possible motives were doubtless at work. To talk about '*the* real motive' in such a connection is an absurdity.

The second fallacy is closely connected with this. After all, whatever motives might be found or suspected among all this collection of individuals, certain results would in fact follow from a successful war against Germany. Poland, Norway, and the rest would be freed from Nazi domination. The persecution of the Jews would cease. Russia would be saved. Even if 'British Imperialism' survived, most people, including the majority of its alleged victims, would admit that to be at least a lesser evil than the alternative of handing over our 'victims' to German rule, which would be the result of non-resistance.* It is open to each of us to decide for himself which of these, or other possible results, he regards as most worth pursuing. But to refrain from any effort to bring about the result that we think to be good, because some of the people with whom we should have to co-operate are more interested in some others of the possible results, would be the height of stupidity. Of course, the situation would be very different if we believed that the results, as a whole, or on balance, of the defeat of Germany would be bad. My personal belief is that the only

---

* We did, however, in the earlier part of the war come across a number of applicants who claimed that we ought to hand over some of our Colonies to Germany in order to secure peace.

genuine and logical conscientious objection on political grounds would be that of a convinced Fascist. For we are unmistakably and avowedly fighting to destroy something that he believes to be good. But the Tribunals have not acted on this view.

There remains one more argument, partly political and partly moral, which by any rational standards must seem extremely odd. That is the kind of argument, with which we have become very familiar, which bases an objection to fighting on the ground of the alleged past misdeeds of this country, particularly in building up its Empire. With the historical truth of these allegations we are hardly concerned here. We did not often discover any evidence that those who put them forward had made any serious study of the facts for themselves. But even supposing that the worst was true, it is very hard to see what the relevance of it is supposed to be. In the case of an individual, if a man has been a hardened criminal, it is not usually supposed that that makes it wrong for him to interpose to prevent a wrong being done by someone else. In fact, if his action results in the prevention of wrong being done to others beside himself, that would be generally considered as going some way to atone for his former crimes.

But, of course, it is not a question of an individual, but of a community, and more particularly of previous generations of the community. A closer analogy would be if it were argued that a man whose great-great-grandfather had owned slaves was thereby morally obliged to allow himself to be carried away into slavery by slave-raiders, if such people existed now. And what is odder still the argument would require that he should equally feel that it was wrong of him to intervene to save anyone else from being carried away into slavery. So far as this line of argument is seriously felt at all, it seems to involve a mystical idea of identity with and responsibility for all the past generations of our community.* I do not believe that this idea can be rationally defended or even formulated. But if there were anything in it, it would surely be the strangest form of expiation to hand over those we were supposed to have wronged to be wronged worse still by the Germans. It is not too much to say that the whole use of this kind of argument is a mark of confusion of thought.†

Besides the political arguments, there is another type of argument which can only be mentioned here. That is the type of religious argument in which the con-

* I have never been able to discover how far back this sense of responsibility is supposed to go. I have not heard anyone drawing any conclusions from the behaviour of our Anglo-Saxon ancestors when they conquered Britain. Perhaps it begins at the Norman Conquest.

† I have seen reason to suspect that, in the minds of some of those who use this type of argument, there is a vague idea that we are fighting this war because we think that Germany is wicked and that therefore we ought to punish her, whereas in fact 'we' have been just as wicked ourselves and have no right to judge. In reality, of course, considerations of this kind do not necessarily come in at all. We are fighting, not primarily to punish Germany, but to prevent her from doing certain things which we regard as evil. The only question we need ask ourselves is whether we regard the state of things that Germany is trying to bring about as so evil that it must be prevented by force if that is the only way.

scientious objection is simply a deduction from certain peculiar, or even eccentric, religious doctrines. Here there could be no argument except a discussion of the grounds for the particular religious view. The doctrine, for instance, of the sect known as Jehovah's Witnesses will seem to most people strange and even fantastic. But, given this religious doctrine, their principle of 'neutrality in all earthly warfare' follows logically enough. But most of the religious objections were not like this, though the precise line of distinction is hard to draw. At least they based their opinions on principles of interpretation of the Scriptures intelligible to the normal person and capable of being rationally discussed. And often, too, they were influenced in their interpretation by general ethical ideas which, again, were possible matters for argument. With such objections we shall be largely concerned in what follows.

We come, then, to the more serious arguments. These take a variety of forms and it is not easy to classify them or set them out in a systematic order. I think, however, that we can distinguish two main lines of approach, which are logically distinct, though, of course, not out of all relation to each other. But that does not mean that in practice they were always kept distinct by those who used them. Not only were they often combined, which is legitimate enough, but they were combined, in many cases, in a way which, as I shall argue, failed to recognise their distinctness or to see their true relation to each other. I shall try to make these points clear in what follows.

NOTE ON DIFFERENCES OF DEGREE

Those who have a taste for precise definition of terms
may possibly complain that I have not used the phrase
'a difference of degree' in its strict and exact sense.
This, up to a point, would be a justifiable criticism.
I have used it in a wider and vaguer sense, because it is
often used in that sense in popular speech, and in
particular in some of the expressions that I have quoted
from other people. I do not think that there is any
danger of misunderstanding in this. Nevertheless, it
may be desirable to append a brief note on this point
where it will not interrupt the main argument.

In the strict sense, I suppose, 'merely a difference of
degree' means a purely quantitative difference in the
amount or degree of a homogeneous material or
quality. Thus, in the instances quoted, the difference
in the amount of strychnine taken or in the rate of
interest charged is purely a difference of degree,
though the results, of course, differ in kind. But in the
wider use the meaning of the phrase is extended to
cover cases where one thing differs from another
qualitatively, but where it is possible to find a whole
series of intermediate cases, each differing from the
next in some small feature, and all these slight differences adding up to a very considerable sum of
differences between the two extremes. That is the only
sense in which, for instance, the difference between the
action of a police force and war could be described as
merely a difference of degree. We may speak of them
as involving the use of different amounts of force. But
'force', in this sense, is not a single homogeneous
thing, like a force in mechanics, with measurable

quantitative differences. It is a name for a number of complicated processes, which differ from each other in various features which cannot be described as simply more or less of the same sort of thing. It is true, however, that one can think of a series of small differences through which, step by step, police action might develop into full-scale war. It is the same with our other instance, the difference in the matter of individual liberty between a tolerant democratic state and a totalitarian dictatorship.

Among all the features in which these cases differ from each other there are doubtless some to which a genuinely quantitative estimate could be applied. For instance, the difference between the number of people affected in one case and another is purely a matter of statistics. But there is always much more in it than that, so it is not *merely* a difference of degree in the strict sense. But the important quantitative estimate that we have to apply in all cases is an estimate of the degree of evil and of good. However we analyse the conceptions of good and evil, it seems a necessary assumption of moral thinking that they differ in degree in different cases, that, for instance, of a number of evil things some will be more evil than others. And when we are faced with alternatives both of which contain some evil we have to attempt an estimate of which is the more evil. This, perhaps, seems so obvious, as not to be worth saying. Yet the numerous conscientious objectors who think they can settle the question by saying that you cannot attain a good end by evil means never seem to have heard of the possibility of being faced with a choice of evils.

CHAPTER II

PACIFISM AS A POLICY

By this phrase I mean, in general terms, the view that no state or community or group of people ought ever under any circumstances to resort to the use of armed force against another group.* So far as this is not based on a supposed immediate moral intuition, beyond the reach of argument, it has to be judged by the standard of human welfare. War is judged by its results and accompaniments, and it is argued that these necessarily, or at any rate in any circumstances that are in fact at all likely to occur, outweigh in evil any results that could arise from not fighting. 'War is the worst evil that can possibly befall humanity', as we have been told more than once. Stress is laid on the obvious evils, moral and material, that war brings with it, both while it is being waged and afterwards. The futility and ineffectiveness of war is particularly emphasised. 'War settles nothing.' 'All wars contain the seeds of more wars in the future.' These are some of the phrases that we most frequently hear. Finally, it is argued that there are alternative methods which can

---

* Of course, the only practical question at issue, particularly in the present connection, is whether one community ought to be pacifist in face of other communities which are not. It should really be hardly necessary to explain this. But some of the more naïve objectors have at times put forward to the Tribunal the—obviously true—statement that if everyone were pacifist there would be no more wars as a ground for some people being pacifist when the rest of the world is not.

meet any situation, more effectively, at the least, than war can. What are we to say about such a position?

That war, in itself, is a very great evil only to be advocated, if at all, as an alternative to an even greater evil may be taken as common ground to all parties. One does not need to be a Pacifist to believe that. But war is a complex phenomenon, and it is very necessary to distinguish between the different elements involved in it if we are to arrive at any sort of estimate of how evil it is, in order to balance it against the evil of possible alternatives. Thus, the loss of life necessarily involved in all wars is an unqualified and irreparable evil. Yet, on the whole, the moral judgement of mankind has never admitted that, either from the point of view of the individual or of the society, life in itself is such a supreme good that everything else should be sacrificed to its preservation and that nothing is worth dying for. At any rate the burden of proof rests on those who maintain that it is. The same applies to the mental and physical suffering, the disablement or loss of health which war brings to so many. It is different with the material destruction and the economic damage caused by war. For, bad though that is, it is not as a rule, except in the case of irreplaceable objects of artistic or historical value, irreparable. It is interesting to note that, if the statisticians are to be believed, the national income in this country which had remained stationary from 1900 to 1914 began to rise again after the war was over, and, with a temporary setback in 1930–1, continued to rise till the outbreak of the present war. It appears, too, that income became more evenly distributed and that the rise was most marked in the lowest income groups.

The whole question of the economic effects of a war is highly complicated and cannot be discussed here. It may suffice to enter a warning against the temptation, to which some pacifist writers seem inclined to yield, to put down everything that happened after the war as the result of the war, or, more indefensibly still, to speak as if everything bad was the result of the war while everything good happened in spite of the war. Thus, one pacifist writer spoke of unemployment as a result of war, on the basis of our own unhappy experience of it, while ignoring the fact that France had no unemployment and Italy hardly any for at least twelve years after the end of the last war. This general warning might well be borne in mind in attempting to estimate the results of war in other fields besides the economic.

But most pacifist writers would probably lay more stress on the moral effects of war. And, in attempting to estimate these, another distinction, which should be obvious but does not appear to be so, should always be borne in mind. That is, the distinction between the effects that show themselves while war is actually being waged and the effects that endure for a prolonged period after the war is over. It is easy to show that many of the moral standards that we most value normally tend to go by the board during a war. It is equally easy to show that, in many cases, war calls out degrees of heroism, devotion and self-sacrifice for which peace gives little opportunity. But it is far more important, in both cases, to know how far these tendencies continue to work afterwards. And here the matter is by no means so obvious. Indeed, one may safely say that there is no good evidence that patterns of behaviour acquired during a war necessarily endure after it is over. There are obvious tendencies working in the opposite direction. For habits that are developed as a response to the stimulus of a particular sort of situation are much less likely to continue when the situation is obviously and entirely altered, as in the transition from war to peace and vice versa, than they are when it is a matter of the small and gradual changes which go on all the time in peace.

One may see an illustration of this in the matter of habituation to the use of violence and the disregard of human life which are necessarily developed in large numbers of people during a war. It is alleged by some pacifist writers, Dr Cadoux among them, that this tendency is carried over from war into peace. Yet the experience of the last war suggests the exact opposite. One of our leading social investigators wrote in 1927: 'Prophecies were freely made during the war to the effect that the population would be brutalised, and that the hundreds of thousands of men who had been trained to attack and kill and take it all in the day's work would not restrain themselves in days of peace. No prophecy seemed on the face of it more reasonable, but no prophecy has been more completely falsified by the event.'*

* *Social Structure of England and Wales*, by Carr-Saunders and Caradog Jones, p. 198. The relevant statistics with regard to crimes of violence are given on the same page.

There is one particular evil that is often charged to the account of war about which a word or two more requires to be said. That is, the supposedly bad effect that war has on our general standards of veracity. 'Truth is the first casualty in war', as the well-known epigram has it. Some years ago Lord Ponsonby published a study of the falsehoods which were given currency during the last war. This was, of course, itself a work of propaganda, and the collection of specific instances that it gave made, at first reading, an impressive effect. But as a serious study it suffered from three cardinal defects.

In the first place, it was no doubt true that a large number of false stories did spring up during the war, from a variety of causes. But simply to collect them together by themselves may give a very false impression. We want to know how typical they were of the state of public opinion in general. How widely were they spread? How many people believed them and for how long? How far were they criticised and corrected? What sort of proportion did they bear to the honest and accurate accounts that were given? We should have to answer all these questions before we could decide how seriously to take these alleged effects of war.

Secondly, we cannot make a sound judgement about these effects without comparing the falsehoods that arise in war with the falsehoods that arise in peace. It would be possible to draw up a most impressive list of these latter from periods of acute political controversy, and also, it must be added, from certain periods of acute religious controversy. The fact is that any strong emotional attachment to a cause tends to lower one's standards of fairness and accuracy. This applies, incidentally, to the cause of peace as much as to any other. When we recall some of the propaganda in the period that preceded the present war we might well feel justified in asserting that Truth could not be the first casualty in the war as she had already been fatally injured in the campaign for peace.

Finally, the book commits the fallacy which has just been discussed of failing to distinguish the effects which appear during a war and cease afterwards from effects that are relatively permanent or, at any rate, endure for some considerable time. The most that Lord Ponsonby's arguments could prove would be that during the excitement of the war there was a certain lowering of standards in this respect. And, regrettable though this would be, it would obviously be very much less serious than a relatively permanent tendency in this direction. And for this no evidence is offered at all. Indeed, I should have thought that it was clearly not the case. This is only one more illustration of how necessary it is in balancing the evils of war against the evils of a possible alternative to consider the probable duration of each as well as their intensity over a limited period.

This brings us to the great weakness of most of the statements of Pacifism as a practical policy. It is easy for them to be eloquent about the obvious evils of war. But all this is beside the point unless it is combined with an equally clear picture of the evils of the alternative in any particular situation. In the circumstances that gave rise to the present war it is clear beyond a doubt that the only possible alternative to fighting was not that piece of wishful thinking 'a peace by negotiation' nor certain concessions of territory or economic privileges but complete subjection to German rule, which, as has been abundantly shown, would claim to control not only political or even economic activities but all intellectual, spiritual and cultural life also. Comparatively few conscientious objectors seem even to have attempted to imagine for themselves what this would mean. In a number of cases we have found them simply refusing to believe, or even to look at the evidence for, any accounts of German oppression or cruelty. Such an attitude is fundamentally as dishonest as a readiness to accept without scrutiny any stories to the discredit of an enemy. Even in the modified form that is to be found in more sophisticated pacifist literature it involves distortion of fact which could be compared with the most violent war propaganda. Other objectors have talked light-heartedly about trying to convert the Germans to Pacifism* or about going on teaching what they believed to be true without, apparently, giving a moment's thought to the question what opportunity they would have of doing that under German rule.

In general, they never seem to ask the question

---

* At the time of the attack on Greece one applicant, on being asked what he thought the Greeks ought to do, replied that they should lay down their arms and try to convert the Germans to Pacifism.

whether the moral and spiritual values which they believe to be threatened by war would not be far more seriously threatened, and over a much longer period, by German domination. Would a high standard of truthfulness be preserved for long under such a rule? Or consider the matter of the growth of hatred and bitterness which is often adduced as one of the special evils of war. There is plenty of reason to think that with most people unresisting subjection to a particularly ruthless and oppressive tyranny is likely to produce a bitterer and more prolonged hatred than fighting. In some cases such an attitude under the stress of long-continued oppression might eventually give place to a kind of masochistic servility and submissiveness. But this is really more destructive of the worth of human personality even than aggressive hatred. It is futile for the Pacifist to reply that he does not want either of these things, and that he advocates submission without either hatred or servility. If he advocates submission as a policy for the nation we must think, not of what a few rare souls may achieve, but of what the effect will in fact be on the great mass of the people. And that is not a matter on which we are free to choose. We can put ourselves, and others, into a situation. But how we and they will come to feel in that situation is, in the main, not in our control.

The more thoughtful Pacifist, however, would probably meet this argument in a different way. He might admit that long-continued oppression or aggression might produce results such as these. But he would pin his faith rather to the possibility of a change of heart in the oppressor or aggressor in response to the attitude that he would have the victims adopt. There are two methods that have been suggested for producing this result, the way of non-violent resistance and the way of non-resistance. These two are often confused, and there is a certain amount of excuse for that in that one may pass into the other by a series of intermediate stages. But they are none the less different and ought to be distinguished.

Non-violent resistance implies an organised refusal to co-operate in any of the work of the country, with the intention of compelling the oppressor to a change of attitude by the discomfort and inconvenience that this causes. This method is particularly associated with the name of Mr Gandhi, but other instances of its use have been quoted by one of its chief advocates, Mr R. B. Gregg, in his book, *The Power of Non-Violence*.

That such a method under certain conditions may be successful no one need deny. Early in the present century the Finns adopted it to meet the Russian threat to their liberties, and for a short time were successful. Another instance, quoted by Mr Gregg, is the success of the Hungarians led by Deák in 1866 in securing the liberty which they had failed to get by fighting in 1848. But this last is really an extraordinary instance for Pacifists to quote, though they evidently believe it supports their case, for it is quoted also by Mr Aldous Huxley in *Ends and Means*, and we heard of it once or twice on the Tribunal. In fact, as is quite obvious, the reason for the susceptibility of the Austrian monarchy to pressure from Hungary was the weakness produced by its defeat at Sadowa. So that force was applied, though not by the Hungarians. Further, the Hungarians, who were about as far from being Pacifists as anyone could be, were ready to offer as a *quid pro quo* the use of force by themselves on the side of Austria against external enemies and against the discontented Slav populations. Mr Gregg and those who followed him would have been well advised to drop this illustration.

In fact, neither the Hungarians nor the Finns have any relevance to the arguments for or against Pacifism at all. Neither of them had any objection of principle to the use of armed force, but, purely as a matter of tactics in the particular circumstances of the time, chose the other method. The Hungarians succeeded. But the Finns succeeded only for the moment against an autocratic Czar standing alone. They failed when he was backed by the strongly nationalistic feeling of the majority of the Duma. And this suggests that non-violent resistance can only succeed against a power which has no very strong motive for going to the lengths necessary to repress it. The experience of India confirms that. For there non-violent resistance was a failure, as Mr Gandhi admitted in his more realistic moments. It did not drive the British out of India. And every attempt to use this method against them has, in the end, developed into the use of violence.

It is often said by the critics of non-violent resistance that, for its successful use, it demands a degree of determination, self-control and unanimity greater than would be required for waging a war, greater, indeed, than one could ever expect to find in any community of normal human people. And that is undoubtedly true. But the criticism can be carried further. For in reality the whole idea of this policy contains an inner contradiction, or at any rate the material for an inner conflict. It demands, on the one side, a resentment or hostility to the aggressor strong enough to lead to concerted and continued resistance, and, on the other, a renunciation of the violence to which these feelings would naturally lead. And these two do not mix well together. Unless the method is immediately successful, it will either turn to violence, if that is practicable, or else to submission and abandonment of resistance. That is the teaching of experience.

The way of non-resistance, on the other hand, lays the emphasis in an entirely different direction. It would not, of course, exclude the possibility of dis-obedience to the oppressor in particular cases where the conscience of individuals told them that an act that they were ordered to do was morally wrong. But that is not what it relies on. There is no suggestion of organised refusal of all obedience or co-operation in order to bend the will of the aggressor by the discom-fort and inconvenience that this would cause him. On the contrary, the emphasis is always on friendliness and good will, and it is argued that a continued display of love and gentleness and charity would, in the end, soften the heart of the aggressor and win him over to more peaceful ways. This will seem to many mere sentimentalism, and, indeed, as the idea was often presented to us, it would deserve to be so characterised. A naïve reliance on love as a sort of magic force capable of doing anything, and an entire lack of knowledge of any relevant example or any clear picture of how it could work in particular circumstances were the most obvious features of this sort of argument. But, as presented by more thoughtful and well-informed Pacifists, this attitude seems to me to be much more realistic than the reliance on non-violent resistance.

It is no part of the case against Pacifism to suppose that everyone is always incurably violent and no one ever restrained by anything but force. There can be no doubt that, under certain conditions, individuals and to some extent communities will respond to love and sympathy and gentleness in a way in which they will not respond to force. Among instances of this, most often quoted by pacifist writers, is the work of Dr Pennell among the wild tribes on the Indian frontier, where his presence was described as worth an army corps as a means of keeping the peace. They also quote the tributes of travellers like Mary Kingsley to the effectiveness of the work of missionaries in West Africa. More pertinent still are the instances of whole communities that have followed the same way with success. The Christians in the Roman Empire faced persecution without resistance, and eventually by the force of their example turned the hearts of their persecutors. The early Quakers in Pennsylvania eschewed the use of force and lived unarmed on the borders of the Indian tribes in perfect safety from the horrors of Indian warfare from which their more militant neighbours suffered. Is it not worth while, the Pacifist asks, always trying this way? It is true that it sometimes fails. But then the use of force sometimes fails also. Let us take the risk.

Such an attitude must have its appeal to everyone. But those who judge these questions in terms of human welfare must realise how great are the things that are at stake. They dare not commit themselves light-heartedly to any risk until they have examined carefully how great it is. They will wish therefore to scrutinise the cases in which such methods have been successful by the side of those in which they have failed. When they do they may well find that it is not a mere toss-up in each case between success and failure but that it is possible to discover something, at any rate, of the conditions under which success is possible and those under which failure is almost certain. And in the latter case no one with any sense of responsibility ought to venture on the risk.

The instances of the individual influence of particular personalities hardly seem relevant at all. The personal achievements of exceptional individuals can hardly be taken as a guide to the policy that a community could safely pursue. In particular, it must be recognised that the activities of such individuals are only possible at all under certain wider conditions which are not under their control. Dr Pennell or the missionaries could not have worked at all in a country under an efficient and ruthless ruler who treated their activities as criminal offences. Even as it was, their work was never tried as a complete substitute for the use of force but rather as a supplement to it. I know of no evidence that they themselves ever suggested that their influence could make all use of force superfluous and that the armed forces could be disbanded. We certainly know of cases in which missionaries have had to be protected by force or the threat of force in the background. It is, therefore, to the actions of communities that we must look for relevant instances.

The case of the Christians under the Roman Empire has often been quoted to us as a proof that the truth could never be suppressed by persecution. Scholars, such as Dr Cadoux, know better. In fact, there never was any serious and prolonged attempt throughout the Empire to extirpate Christianity, nor, in spite of occasional outbursts of mob violence, was there any widespread and deep-rooted hatred of Christianity among the general population. The most that can be claimed is that the patience and meekness of Christians under such persecution as there was did do a good deal to win over many people to the faith. And that may readily be granted. On the other hand, it must be remembered that the Roman imperial world was favourable ground for the spread of Christianity. People were eagerly searching for a new and satisfying religion, and many religions were being tried. Further, in the period of the most rapid spread of Christianity, there were many dangers and sufferings and misfortunes which made the inhabitants no longer confident or sure of themselves, and ready to turn to any faith that might give support and consolation. Even so, there is reason to doubt whether Christianity would have finally triumphed if it had not secured the support of the established government, before, in all probability, it had won over the majority of the population. This support eventually developed into the forcible suppression of paganism.

What is, perhaps, more significant is that Christianity never converted the Roman world to a belief in Pacifism. There were no fewer wars after Constantine than before. Some Pacifists criticise the Christian Church for this, and argue that this was the point at which Christianity took the wrong turning. But it might equally well be argued that this merely shows a realisation of the plain fact that a doctrine which can be pursued by a small and isolated sect, in a world in which law and order and public safety are looked after by other authorities, cannot be applied in the same way by those who are prepared to make themselves responsible for the welfare of the whole community.

The Quakers in Pennsylvania are another matter. But a careful examination of their history does not warrant the confident and sweeping conclusions that are drawn from it by some Pacifists. It is clear that a good many Indians, at any rate, were not at first aggressively inclined towards the settlers, and were quite ready to secure benefits from trading with them. The early Swedish settlers in Delaware, for instance, though far from pacifist, were on the best of terms with the Indians. What made these latter so aggressive, in many cases, was the extremely unscrupulous way in which they were cheated and exploited by the British settlers. The one community that behaved with strict fairness and honesty towards the Indians naturally did not arouse this resentment. It might be mentioned, however, that Pennsylvania as a whole was never entirely disarmed and defenceless. There were armed forces within the colony raised from the non-Quaker settlers. And, of course, the neighbouring colonies would have had some interest in preventing the entire destruction of a settlement. It is curious to notice that, when it was a question of possible war, not with the Indians but with the French, the Quakers appealed to this fact in their arguments with the royal governor to show that there was no urgent reason to press them to bear arms.

What is of much more significance, however, is that, however successful the Quakers were in disarming the hostility of the Indians, they failed entirely with their fellow-Christians. In the middle of the eighteenth century, gangs of truculent Scotch-Irish Presbyterians, nurtured on the teaching of the Old Testament that it was the duty of the chosen people to kill off the heathen, rose in arms in the main to assert their right to ill-treat the Indians as much as they liked. In this crisis the Quakers had themselves to take up arms before peace and order were re-established.* We may note also, that, though the Quaker method may, up to a point, have secured immunity for themselves, there is no evidence at all that this had any effect in inspiring other communities (e.g. the Indian tribes in

* See *The Quaker Colonies* by S. G. Fisher published in the 'Chronicles of America' series by the Yale University Press.

their relations to each other) to follow their example
and adopt their methods.

That is a significant instance of the failure of an
attitude of good will and gentleness to touch the hearts
of an aggressive people. But it does not stand alone.
The natives in some of the West Indian islands, when
Columbus and his successors first landed there, were,
by all accounts, gentle, friendly, hospitable people who
hardly knew what fighting was. Yet so far were they
from winning over the invaders that the brutal exploi-
tation to which the Spaniards subjected them ended in
the extinction of the whole race. Christianity made
great progress in Japan in the sixteenth and seven-
teenth centuries. The Japanese Christians seem to have
had many of the virtues of the early Christians. At any
rate under persecution they displayed the same quali-
ties of steadfastness in the faith and Christian charity
towards their persecutors. But this did not deter the
rulers of Japan when they decided to suppress Christianity, and they carried on the work of persecution
with the utmost brutality and thoroughness until
Christianity ceased to exist in Japan. The Jews, though
Judaism is not a pacifist religion, have practised non-
resistance as a policy almost since the Dispersion. But
this has not saved them from centuries of recurrent
persecution, culminating in the bestialities of the present German government, which has every prospect
of annihilating the whole race in the lands under
German control. The same fate would doubtless befall
the German Pacifists, who, so far from disarming the
hostility of the Nazi movement, seem to have been

the special objects of brutality in the concentration camps.

Two experiments in Christian Pacifism, separated from each other by a wide period of time, deserve special notice. In the nineteenth century the Methodist missionaries in Fiji began by teaching an uncompromising Pacifism as an integral part of the Christian doctrine. At first they made some progress, though it seems clear that other motives, besides the attraction of the Gospel teaching, played their part in this. But, as the threat to the established customs of the natives became clear, hostility developed and before long began to take the form of active attack. The missionaries themselves were never entirely without protection owing to the presence from time to time of ships of the British navy. But their native converts were exposed to a series of assaults, and so far were they from disarming hostility by their attitude that their refusal to fight made them an easy prey to the enemy. It became clear that Christianity in the Fiji Islands was facing the prospect of absolute extinction, as had happened in other islands. And the missionaries slowly and reluctantly began to abandon their absolute Pacifism and to encourage their converts to take up arms to defend themselves. But the danger still continued, and the turning point only came when King George, the Methodist ruler of Tonga, came to their help at the head of a band of chosen warriors. The heathen natives were decisively defeated at the Battle of Kamba in 1855, and from that time Christianity went forward by leaps and bounds. The whole story is told in detail by Prof. G. C. Henderson in his book, *Fiji and the Fijians*.

The history of the Anabaptists in the Reformation period is instructive, particularly as the lessons to be drawn from it are not, at first sight, at all simple or obvious. This sect, as it first developed, was predominantly completely pacifist in creed, though there were certain communities within it which did not take this attitude. But this peacefulness and gentleness did not save them from the most savage persecution. Under the stress of this some of them took up arms, though they were not in a situation in which this gave any hope of success.* But large numbers remained pacifist and faced the persecution without any attempt at resistance. The Pacifist is entitled to point out that the sect managed to survive, though in depleted numbers, in spite of all this, and at last attained some degree of toleration in practice. But how did they survive? There seems to have been a variety of reasons, but it is clear that it was not to any extent due to the conversion of those who persecuted them to any sympathy with their views. It was the toleration of indifference rather than sympathy. And this was largely due to their obscurity and unobtrusiveness. It is worth pointing out how much easier it would be for scattered communities of this kind to live on in the conditions

* The Pacifist who is inclined to draw conclusions favourably to his case from the fact that the Anabaptists who resisted were exterminated might consider the case of their fellow-heretics the Waldenses, who, at certain periods, undoubtedly owed their survival to the vigorous and successful resistance that, under favourable geographical conditions, they were able to put up.

of the sixteenth century than it would be to-day, when modern means of communication and dissemination of news would make it impossible for them to remain for long unnoticed and undetected. The further development is interesting, too. For as they achieved some measure of toleration in practice, they tended to cease to be pacifist. There were many Anabaptists in Cromwell's army. And their modern descendants, the Baptists, are not a pacifist body, though there is a pacifist minority among them.

The conclusion of all this seems inevitable—that a Christian pacifist attitude can never be effective against those who meet it with a definite rival creed of their own, which inspires and satisfies them, particularly when that creed leads them to success by its standards. It is futile to talk as if there was something so inherently attractive about Christian Pacifism to all types of temperament that it was bound to prevail. It is a great weakness of many Pacifists that they are so deeply convinced of the truth of their belief that they feel that it must really have a superior appeal to any rival creed, and that the adherents of the rival creed cannot truly believe in it as deeply and fervently as the Pacifists do in theirs. There is nothing in experience to justify such a supposition. It seems, then, that the most that the Christian Pacifists in face of a really aggressive opponent could hope for—and that with no great confidence—would be that they might so disarm hostility as to be allowed to exist as a small tolerated sect, a refuge for a minority of peculiar temperament, on the condition that they should renounce all responsibility for and all attempts to influence the general direction of the affairs of the larger community.*

This illustrates a weakness, which has already been mentioned, in even the best of the presentations of Pacifism as a possible policy for a national state. That is the failure to see clearly the difference between what is possible for a small voluntary society, which only those who feel wholeheartedly in sympathy with its views need join, and a wider compulsory society, such as a state, which has to include every kind of person within a given area of the most varied views and temperaments. And there is a more particular issue involved here. Christian Pacifism, or indeed any kind of Pacifism, cannot be considered merely as a practical policy, but involves a whole change of heart and the adoption of a completely new spirit and attitude. Indeed, a pacifist policy in practice without the attainment by the great majority of those concerned of a completely pacifist state of mind would give us the worst of both worlds and could only be the most complete failure. Yet the attainment of a state of mind is not a policy in the sense in which we generally use the term. It certainly could not be discussed and decided by democratic methods at a General Election. And the thoughtful Pacifist might be invited to consider the situation that would arise if a pacifist government were elected by a bare majority, in which there

* That would certainly involve the renunciation of any right of criticism of the actions of the rulers, and probably of any attempt at proselytising.

would inevitably be many who were momentarily attracted by all sorts of motives other than a completely pacifist state of mind, while a strong minority remained entirely opposed to the whole doctrine. I venture to suggest that a pacifist government, if it were to survive as such at all, would find itself driven rapidly along the road to complete totalitarianism. For it could hardly tolerate behaviour, or even propaganda, contrary to pacifist principles if it was to have any chance of success for its policy.

There is a further point. Any policy which demands a change of heart and a conversion to a new attitude of mind in large numbers of people can only be a long-term policy. And it can only be pursued at all if certain conditions exist which make it possible. But if these conditions are threatened the long-term policy cannot by itself meet the immediate threat. Some Pacifists would claim that in the very long run even the conditions that made the threat would cease to be operative. That is a matter of faith, not of argument. But, in any case, it seems a very perverted moral point of view to regard with equanimity the existence of a preventible evil for a long period, perhaps for centuries, because it is believed that it will eventually die out.

It remains, then, to deal briefly with the pacifist counter-attack on the ineffectiveness and futility of war. The retort to those who point out the failures of Pacifism, that the use of force also sometimes fails, does not take us very far. The non-pacifist is only too well aware of that. But he is in an essentially different position from the Pacifist, for he is not advocating the use of force as a universal principle or a good in itself, but as one possible means to an end, only to be used if there is a reasonable chance of success and if no other means are available. These conditions are to some extent calculable, and, though there will always remain the possibility of mistake as in all human affairs, it is at least possible to be saved from committing oneself to the use of force when there is clearly very little chance of these conditions being fulfilled.

But the more sweeping pacifist slogan—too sweeping for some of the more reasonable Pacifists—'Wars settle nothing', is, if it is taken to mean what it says, a simple and obvious absurdity. It would be far truer to say that every war settles something. The fact that our language and institutions are English, and neither Welsh nor Anglo-Saxon, was settled by war. War decided that Rome and not Carthage was to be the mistress of the Mediterranean world, with all that that implied for future civilisation. The frontiers between Christianity and Mohammedanism were, in the main, settled by war, and have proved impervious to all peaceful missionary effort. War decided that Spain was not to rule in Holland nor the Turks over the Christian states of the Balkans. It decided that Canada was to be a British not a French dominion, that the United States was to be an independent Republic, and that it was to be one Republic, and not two or more. And the list could be multiplied indefinitely. Indeed, it would be hard to find a statement that is more decisively refuted by the facts of history.

Hypothetical arguments about what might have

happened if people had behaved differently do not demand much attention. If it were argued that the same results could have been achieved, in those circumstances, without fighting then it would plainly be untrue. If it were argued that better results could have been attained, we must be careful to avoid ambiguity. If everyone everywhere was a Christian Pacifist or if no one wanted anything strongly enough to fight for it, very likely things would have been much better. But the supposition is too remote from any realities even to have much meaning. If, on the other hand, it were meant that it would have had better effects if one side had always refused to fight so that the side that was prepared to fight had had its way, we are still in the region of unprovable hypothesis, and we should need far more details to be filled in by the imagination before we could even argue it. For one thing, it would make a good deal of difference which side was supposed to have given way. But the more one thinks about it the more impossible does it become to base any rational argument on such imaginary hypotheses. Certainly in some of these cases a good many other suppositions would have to be made to make the contention even plausible.

There is reason to suspect that the obviously false proposition that wars settle nothing has been confused in the minds of many Pacifists with the quite different proposition that no war settles everything. At least so one would judge from the number of arguments produced at the Tribunal which implied that the war could not be justified unless by itself without any further effort on anyone's part it would automatically solve all difficulties and, in particular, bring about a state of perpetual peace.* Of course no sane person would ever claim that any war could do that. Obviously new problems will always be arising, and new efforts will be called for all the time to deal with them satisfactorily. But that does not alter the fact that, in certain circumstances, the conditions which make it possible to deal with them satisfactorily could only be secured by war. And that, if it is correct, would be sufficient to justify the non-pacifist's position.

As for the more specific charge that wars always lead to further wars because of the legacy of hatred and bitterness that they leave behind them, it is difficult to

---

* This seems to be at the back of the great play that many conscientious objectors make with the phrase 'a war to end war', as applied to the last war. I suppose the argument, which they evidently feel is of great weight, is that the last war was entered upon to end war—they sometimes assert this in set terms—it failed, and therefore no war can end war. In fact, the last war, like the present one, was not entered on to end war but to prevent certain definite evils from happening. After it was started, someone coined the phrase, 'Let us make this a war to end war'. But obviously that was not intended to suggest that winning the war by itself would be enough to end all wars. Clearly that was a matter for future policy, and the fact that we failed once is neither an argument that we must necessarily always fail nor that we ought to allow the specific evils we are fighting against to have their way. I might add, here, a further point that ending the war by the adoption of Pacifism, even if that adoption could be general, would not necessarily guarantee us against any more wars in the future, unless we assume that Pacifism, once adopted, would never be abandoned by subsequent generations. This assumption is in fact generally made by Pacifists. But no grounds are ever given for it, and it is certainly not self-evidently true.

find any historical basis for such a sweeping generalisation. People are so obsessed by the supposed example of Germany and the present war that they forget that twenty years ago we ourselves were at war with Turkey, and that now we are almost allies. The American Civil War, though it left some bitterness for a number of years, has not resulted in any further war. We have had a hundred and thirty years of peace with the United States since the last war. The South African war has not led to another war. It is true that there is still some racial ill-feeling there. But that was among the causes rather than the results of the war and diminished rather than increased after it. The Maori wars a century ago have resulted in perfectly happy and harmonious relations between British and Maoris. A hundred years ago there was a civil war in Switzerland which has produced a completely united and contented nation. And the list might be multiplied indefinitely. Anyone given to historical generalisations might produce instances to support the view that a really complete and unmistakable defeat is the surest way of making a nation peaceful in the future. But, in fact, none of these generalisations are really decisive.

Perhaps a word might be said about the relation between the last war and the present one, not because of any real logical relevance to the discussion, but because of the constancy with which it reappears in a certain type of pacifist argument. 'The present war is the direct result of the last one' is a phrase which we have heard repeated on numerous occasions. By itself such a phrase is too vague to have very much meaning.

But a more serious attempt to give some specific content to it is made by those who trace the present war to the bitterness caused by the Treaty of Versailles, which led to the rise of the Nazi movement. In some presentations of the argument it is possible to trace the further unspoken assumption that, once the war had been started, it was inevitable that the treaty which ended it would be as unjust and oppressive as the Treaty of Versailles was.

The relevance of this question to the duty of fighting Nazi Germany is not really very great. For anyone who believes that the results of the triumph of Hitlerism would be of incalculable evil, and that they can only be prevented by fighting, his duty to fight is not in the least affected by past events. A well-known foreign writer once suggested that if we were faced by a homicidal maniac, whose mania had been aggravated by our mistaken treatment of him in the past, the fact that we were partly responsible for his condition would not be regarded by any sane person as a reason why we should allow him to kill ourselves, still less other people for whom we were responsible. Analogies are dangerous things, but this one seems of more validity than they generally possess.

But, putting this aside, the assertion that the present war was the result of the Treaty is itself not free from ambiguity. Does it mean that, given the Treaty, whatever policy had been pursued afterwards would still have resulted in the rise of Hitler and the present war? Or does it mean that, given the Treaty, the policy which was pursued subsequently was the only one that could have been pursued? We seem to be trenching here on the metaphysical problem of the Freedom of the Will which is better left for discussion elsewhere. But it is interesting to note that the Pacifists, who seem inclined to postulate absolute freedom of choice in the results that would follow from the adoption of a pacifist policy, lean towards an absolutely deterministic doctrine of fatalism and inevitability when it is a question of the results of war.

It would be out of place to attempt a discussion of the nature and effects of the Treaty of Versailles here. Most people would now recognise that the explanation of war in general, and this war in particular, would have to be looked for in something much deeper or more complex than a single, simple factor like this. Even as a proximate cause the influence of the grievances against the Treaty as an incentive to the rise of Nazism has, in the past, been greatly exaggerated. Hitler has himself described the difficulties that he experienced in rousing German feeling on the subject. It is, I suppose, arguable that, at the time Hitler rose to power, the issues were so nicely balanced that any change in what went before would have turned the scales the other way. Whether that would have meant that there would have been no war is another matter, but at least it would have been a war of a different character. Alternatively, it might equally be argued that if the Treaty had been more severe and Germany further weakened or kept in subjection there would have been no Hitler. But, in any case, most observers agree that the major cause in creating an atmosphere favourable to Hitlerism was the economic crisis. It was part of the propaganda of the Nazis to proclaim the Treaty as the cause of the sufferings of the German people. It is natural for everyone to welcome a scapegoat. But that could have been done just as effectively whatever form the Treaty had taken.

Further, it is relevant to point out that Hitler was not an isolated phenomenon. Italy set the example, both of totalitarian dictatorship and aggression against other states. And Italy was not a defeated power, though it is true that she did not gain as much as she would have liked. But the first example of large-scale aggression was given by Japan, also something approaching a totalitarian state, and Japan was not only not a defeated power, but was hardly more than formally a belligerent. Japan is, indeed, a striking example of the way in which a taste for aggression grows with success in it. There is no doubt that the example of Japan's successful aggression had a good deal of influence in Germany and still more, perhaps, in Italy.

To return to the main issue. The upshot of the preceding argument is that the Pacifist has entirely failed to make out a case for denying the commonsense view that partial or one-sided Pacifism, either within a country or between countries, means the domination of the more violent and aggressive elements, with all the evils that that brings. He has equally failed to produce any rational grounds for the belief that these elements are in the least likely to be converted from their belief in violence and aggres-

INTERNATIONAL CHRISTIAN
GRADUATE UNIVERSITY

sion by anything that the Pacifist can do or say. If these arguments are sound, therefore, it is clear that by any standard of social or individual welfare on earth, human happiness, the reign of justice, even the establishment of good will between men, absolute Pacifism as a policy cannot be defended. And anyone who takes any degree of responsibility for the political ordering of the world is bound to accept to some degree the standard of human welfare. But there still remains for consideration the position of those who maintain that, for the conscience of individuals, there are standards of absolute right and wrong, not dependent on the results, at any rate in this world, and that these standards tell them as a matter of individual duty that it would be wrong for them to fight. It is this position, in its various forms, that we must now consider.

CHAPTER III

PACIFISM AS AN INDIVIDUAL DUTY

This position represents a fundamentally different attitude from the other. But that is not to say that they are out of all relation with each other, and it is important to see clearly what the true relation between the two points of view is.

Obviously, if everyone, or the great majority in any country, adopted the point of view of Pacifism as a personal duty, that country would have to adopt Pacifism as a policy in some form or other. What form that policy would have to take is a difficult and complicated question, and raises many problems to which Pacifists do not seem to have given much serious thought. To mention only one, what would be the attitude of a pacifist majority to a non-pacifist minority? On the other hand, it must be admitted that those who emphasise the personal duty regardless of consequences, might well feel justified in declining to attempt to frame a general policy until the need for such a policy came a little closer to the realm of practical possibilities. There are some, indeed, who would maintain, with a good deal of justification, that their attitude, as far as could be humanly foreseen, never would in fact be adopted by more than a small minority.

A much more important question is whether the connection between the two points of view works the other way. In other words, does the advocacy of Pacifism as a policy for a country necessarily involve that those who advocate it should refuse to take part in a war, once their policy has been rejected and the war has actually begun? It is really quite clear that there is no logical connection. An objection to making war at all is not the same thing as an objection to taking part in a war, once it has been started, and those Pacifists who identify the two, or give the one as an adequate reason for the other, are displaying a serious confusion of thought. In their advocacy of Pacifism as a policy for a nation they are accepting the appeal to the consequences of a course of action as determining, at any rate in part, whether it should be pursued or not. But when they are considering their own course of action, they do not consider the consequences of their refusal to take part in the war, once it has broken out and there is no prospect of a speedy end to it, but instead base their argument on the hypothetical consequences of a course of action—the avoidance of war altogether—which has not in fact been taken. It is difficult to see any logic in this.

It is clear that the first and most obvious effect of the action of the conscientious objector would be to weaken the British war effort, and that is, indeed, the object which some of them clearly proclaim. But they are much less clear about the consequences which would follow from this. It is obvious that it would do nothing to put an end to the war, and nothing to diminish the evil consequences of war. One possible result would be to make a German victory more likely.

The only other possible result, if it did not succeed in doing that, would be to postpone our victory and make the war, with all its evils, last longer. Those Pacifists who are prepared, in any degree, to accept the responsibility for the obvious consequences of their actions are shirking the issue if they are not prepared to say definitely whether they regard these consequences, the victory of Germany or the prolongation of the war, as desirable or not. And if they admit that they are not desirable they are under an obligation to state what other consequences they think that their action in the present circumstances will produce, which are so desirable that they outweigh the evils of these. A few applicants before the Tribunal to whom we succeeded in conveying this point expressed a vague hope that their present attitude will have the effect of increasing the number of Pacifists in the future. On what grounds they thought this, how long they thought it would take until this had attained sufficient dimensions to prevent war altogether, whether they thought the vague prospect of this in the remote future could outweigh the obviously evil results of their action here and now—all these points were left in obscurity. But it was comparatively rare to find an objector who would even face the question at all. The constant tendency was to bring back the discussion to the general evils of war.

This confusion of the issues is particularly characteristic of the Peace Pledge movement. The original intention of this movement was to make war impossible. It was argued that if a sufficient number of people refused to participate in a war no government would be able to start one. It failed in that object. And when a course of action is undertaken in order to produce a certain result, it would normally be considered quite irrational to persist in it when it had clearly failed to produce that result and was, instead, producing results which those who undertook the action would not regard as desirable. But, of course, in this case the matter was prejudged by the pledge which was taken. One sympathises with the moral dilemma of those who took a solemn pledge in order to produce a certain result and felt that they were bound to hold to it even when it became clear that it had failed in its purpose. The only conclusion is that no one ought to put himself in such a position and that pledges of this kind are morally unjustifiable. As a clear-sighted pacifist friend said to me, the Peace Pledge was really a piece of bluff. And, when the bluff was called, those who attempted it found themselves in a position which could not be rationally defended. We may well wonder whether the generous and impulsive originator of the movement would have found himself altogether comfortable with its present representatives.

At any rate, it ought to be clear beyond a doubt that a belief that war is such an evil that no nation under any circumstances ought to take part in it, does not by itself give any guide to the right course to be taken by those individuals who hold such a view once war has broken out. An eminent divine is reported to have declared himself 'pacifist up to the outbreak of war'.

And some more persistent Pacifists have attempted to make merry at his expense. But in reality his view is much more logical and defensible than theirs.

We come now to the real subject of this section, the views of those who maintain that they feel an imperative obligation as individuals not to take part in any war-like activities, and that this obligation is absolute, irrespective of consequences either to themselves or to anyone else. This is conscientious objection in the strict sense of the term, and, as such, the country has recognised that it is to be respected. But respecting a position and admitting its validity are two different things, and it is with the latter that we are now concerned.

It has long been a matter for discussion among moral philosophers whether any action can be pronounced absolutely right or wrong regardless of its consequences. On the one side, it may be argued that actions do in fact have consequences, sometimes very serious ones, and that we cannot ignore them in judging whether the action should be done or not. To do so would be a vain attempt to evade our responsibility for the natural consequences of our actions. On the other, it may be asked, if our actions are to be judged by their consequences, by what test are the consequences to be judged? By their consequences again? If so, we seem to be started on an infinite process, which will never lead us to any final ground for moral judgement of our actions. Further, the consequences of any action are themselves infinite, and a great many of them necessarily beyond our knowledge. We must, at some point, arrive at something which we can say is good or bad absolutely. These are only illustrations of the complicated considerations which the question gives rise to. It would obviously be out of place to attempt a discussion of them here. All that needs to be said is that weighty authority could be quoted on either side, and we certainly cannot simply dismiss the view that certain actions may be judged right or wrong irrespective of the consequences.

That does not, however, mean that we must accept it in any particular case. On the contrary, such a claim demands particularly careful scrutiny. And the first step in this is to inquire from what source such a judgement is supposed to derive its authority. In the present case we find that, broadly speaking, there are two main grounds on which it is based. In the first place, it is sometimes asserted as an immediate moral intuition. This was comparatively rarely put forward as a sufficient justification in itself, but was more frequently found in combination with the second. This, which was characteristic of the great majority of conscientious objectors, was based on the authority of some religious doctrine, particularly, of course, of one form or another of Christianity.

A claim to an immediate intuition is not open to direct argument. But that does not mean that it is to be lightly dismissed as unworthy of serious consideration. In my view, some kind of immediate intuition is the basis on which, or the material from which, all morality is built up. When it is genuinely what it claims to be it takes the form of a close, and possibly unique, combination of an emotional reaction and an intellectual judgement in the presence of a concrete situation when an actual choice of actions is before us. That is what I have described elsewhere as 'first-hand moral experience', and without it there is no genuine morality. When at the Tribunal we had before us a simple, unlettered applicant who has had little more to say than 'I just couldn't do it', I often felt more certain of the reality of the moral conviction than when listening to some of the most skilful and elaborate arguments of the more sophisticated intellectuals.

But though, as I should maintain, such an immediate judgement is a genuine part of moral experience, that is not to say that it is infallible. In fact, nothing is more certain than that what seem, to those who have them, the most certain moral intuitions, may be wrong. That is proved by the fact that moral intuitions differ from one person to another, and what is more, that the same person may modify or abandon a belief which at one time seemed to him absolutely certain. That is not to say, as some of the more hasty critics of conscientious objectors are inclined to do, that the objector ought to ignore what he believes his conscience tells him because it may be mistaken. The objector is perfectly justified in replying that, though he may be wrong, he can only make up his own mind as best he can and act on that. But it does mean that he has a duty to scrutinise these alleged dictates of his conscience very carefully with a full realisation of the possible sources of error.

One source of error is the possible confusion between the specifically moral feeling and other feelings. In particular, when it is a question of taking human life or using violence, the moral revulsion from such an action must not be confused with a purely physical or nervous revulsion. I would not question that the two are different and can be distinguished by careful scrutiny. But there is no doubt that they can be, and sometimes are, confused. We felt, for instance, that there were very strong grounds for thinking that such a confusion had been made by one applicant at the Tribunal who emphasised his objection to taking human life by saying that he felt just the same about animal life, and added that he always got someone else to do the killing of animals for him on the farm.

A more profound source of error lies in the possibility that the nature of the action itself and of the concrete situation in which it takes place has been imperfectly or incorrectly envisaged by the person concerned. He may have perceived only certain more obvious features and failed to realise other aspects of it which are just as relevant to its moral worth. In other words, it might be that his moral reaction would have been the right one if the action was as he saw it or was all he saw in it, but was in fact wrong because the action, in its actual situation, was other than or more than he realised. That is, in fact, what I suppose that non-pacifists, who would admit the weight that should be attached to these moral intuitions, would say was wrong with the Pacifist's attitude. His moral revulsion comes from seeing clearly certain aspects of the situation, which would, if they were all there was in it, justify the attitude, and from failing to see or to visualise sufficiently clearly other aspects which, when they are taken into account, put an entirely different face on the matter.

But I think the criticism would have to go deeper. This direct moral experience is, in my view at any rate, a reality. And it bears testimony to the fact that an action, or course of action, is not to be judged *merely* by its consequences but has a moral quality, positive or negative, of its own. But none the less an action does have consequences and accompaniments, and these cannot be ignored in the final decision as to whether it is to be done or not. It needs some thought and investigation to discover these; they are not given in immediate inspection. And therefore the first moral revulsion from or attraction to an action, while it must be taken into account, cannot be regarded as the final arbiter of our decision when the immediate choice of actions lies before us.

A further complication arises when we begin to examine the matter a little further and ask what 'an action' is. Where do we draw the line which distinguishes 'an action' from its consequences or accompaniments? In fact, we shall find that what we mean by 'an' action in ordinary speech varies according to the object of the discussion in which we use the phrase. 'An' action is, in reality, a section cut off arbitrarily to suit our immediate purposes from a continuous and complicated stream of events. Thus the conscientious objector speaks of killing a man as 'an action', and says it is wrong regardless of the reasons for it or the consequences of it. Would it not be equally or more correct to say that the action was pressing the trigger of a rifle and that the death of the man was the consequence of this? In this case the action is being judged right or wrong by its consequences, not in itself. Why, therefore, draw a sharp line at those consequences and refuse to consider the further consequences involved? No doubt these will seem unworthy subtleties to those who prefer feeling about things to thinking about them. But these subtleties are really relevant to the position now under discussion, and if those who adopt it could bring themselves to think out the full implications they would often have to modify their points of view.

At any rate, enough has been said to indicate how it is possible to view with respect these immediate ethical intuitions, which is what I think most people mean in speaking of their 'consciences', and regard them as a real moral contribution, and at the same time refuse to allow them final or infallible authority. To treat this point further would involve a detailed argument on ethical principles which would take us beyond the scope of the present discussion. But we may feel justified in leaving the matter here because this appeal to the moral consciousness as the sole and sufficient ground for conscientious objection is characteristic of only a very small minority of the objectors who have been before us. Much more often it appears, if at all, as subordinate to religious considerations. A very great majority of objectors base their objection fundamentally on the teaching of Christianity, and use these moral considerations, if at all, as merely an aid to the interpretation or application of the Christian teaching. In general this is quite a legitimate procedure. We most of us take over a good many of our moral beliefs from others, from some authoritative teacher or some organised body of belief. But, if we genuinely adopt them, we do not merely receive them passively at second-hand. They only have any meaning for us and are only accepted because there is something in our own moral experience which responds to them. On the other hand, we should never have seen what was implied in our own moral experience or have been able to draw these conclusions out of it unless it had been suggested to us by the teaching which we follow. Anyone who wishes to interpret and apply the teaching of the New Testament to our own time must, to a greater or lesser degree, use this method of linking up this teaching with his own moral experience. But that must, of course, be combined with a serious effort at historical understanding of the situation to which that teaching was first applied.

What are we to say, then, of the pacifist interpretation of the teaching of Christ and his immediate followers as recorded in the New Testament?* Some

---

* I should, perhaps, explain, in connection with the discussion which follows, that I do not myself approach this question from the point of view of the orthodox Christian, who necessarily takes the teaching of Christ as a final and absolutely true guide to action. But I am deeply concerned to understand what the teaching of Christ, as a great moral and religious teacher, really was. And I can at least claim that this frees me

of the more extreme critics of Pacifism seem to make it a ground of reproach that it attempts any interpretation of this at all. Professor Hearnshaw, in a very intemperate attack in the *Hibbert Journal*, accused the Pacifists of picking and choosing what suits their case from the teaching of the Gospels. Such criticism is quite unwarranted. So far as it applies at all, it applies just as much to anyone at the present day who believes that the teaching of Christ has any application at all to our own behaviour in our own circumstances. He must exercise some degree of discrimination and selection. There have been occasional individuals who attempted to escape from this necessity altogether. In the Middle Ages, for instance, it is said that one could meet people going through life maimed because they took quite literally the command, 'If thy hand offend thee, cut it off'. And to those who protested that the words cannot have been meant as literally as all that they doubtless replied that that would be picking and choosing what suits ourselves from the Gospels. But the consensus of Christian opinion, even the most fundamentalist, at the present day would certainly be against them. In this respect Pacifists and non-pacifists are in exactly the same position. Neither can dispose of the other by such cheap and easy methods.

It would be generally recognised—though the implications of this are not always clearly seen—that

from any temptation to force the interpretation of Christ's words in order to be able to claim their support for views at which I have arrived myself on other grounds.

the recorded words of Christ or the apostles were in every case addressed to actual people, living in particular conditions and with particular problems of their own in mind, which are never quite the same as ours. Indeed, unless the teaching had been intelligible to those who heard it and felt by them to be applicable to their own problems, it could never have been received or preserved at all. We cannot, therefore, expect to find a direct and specific answer to our own particular problems. Even the most fundamentalist interpreter has, at some point, to pass beyond the question what Christ actually said to the question what he would have said. And that is always a matter of inference, involving interpretation in other terms, selection, and emphasis on this or that. Every Christian body has, in practice, recognised the need for such a process, whether it has entrusted it to an infallible Church, to a Church with a degree of authority short of infallibility, or to the personal judgement of individual Christians. It is, of course, only in so far as the last point of view is adopted that the possibility of an argument on the subject, such as is attempted here, arises.

What would Christ have said about participation in warfare in a situation like the present, unlike anything with which he was faced in his own experience? We are safe in saying that in no circumstances would he have wished for war or welcomed it if it came or been satisfied with a situation which gave rise to war. In that general sense, the much used phrase that warfare is 'contrary to the mind of Christ' is obviously true.

But that does not take us very far. Telling lies would also, I suppose, be contrary to the mind of Christ. Yet, as the stock dilemmas of the text-books of ethics show, there are possible occasions on which to tell a lie would, in the judgement of nearly all serious thinkers, be not only excusable but a positive duty.*

An outstanding fact, which Pacifists seem to skate over very lightly, is that neither Christ nor his immediate disciples make any mention of war, though there were certainly opportunities for doing so if it had been intended that the Christian teaching was to be regarded as absolutely forbidding participation in warfare in all circumstances. Both Christ, when he healed the centurion's servant, and Peter, when he baptised Cornelius, came into contact with professional soldiers. And it would surely be very queer, if their profession was regarded as absolutely incompatible with Christian belief, that no suggestion to this effect was ever made. We may contrast this with the relatively numerous and quite definite statements about the difficulty of reconciling the possession of wealth with

* The most familiar of these instances is the supposed case of an innocent man pursued by murderers whose life could only be saved by a timely lie. Another one is the old story of the theatre manager who, when a fire broke out behind the scenes, in order to avoid a panic came before the curtain and told the audience some concocted story—I believe that in the original version it was that the Queen (for it dates from Victorian times) had died suddenly—which induced them to leave the theatre in a quiet and orderly fashion, thus saving hundreds of lives. I would commend these instances to the consideration of Pacifists who say that you cannot attain a good end by bad means.

a true Christian life. One can hardly doubt that Christ's teaching is far more specific and unmistakable on this point than on the question of warfare.

Many Pacifists would argue in reply that Christ himself set the example by renouncing warfare as a means of establishing the Kingdom of God on earth. And some would add that this was the reason for his loss of popularity among the Jews who were expecting him to lead them in revolt against the Romans. This last is pure conjecture with no warrant in the text. But, in any case, no valid conclusion seems to follow from what Christ decided on in the special circumstances of that time. Obviously, armed revolt against the Romans would have been a hopeless enterprise which could only have led to the end of any chance of spreading Christian teaching at all. Later, of course, St Paul saw clearly that the one thing that would be absolutely fatal to nascent Christianity would be to come into conflict with the Roman power, which was always inclined to toleration but would naturally resist any direct attack on its own authority. That is why he laid such stress on the duty of respect for the powers that be. But no conclusion can be drawn from this about what the Christian's duty would be in very different circumstances. One may add, what is perhaps too obvious to need saying, that no genuine religious teacher would, in any case, advocate the use of force while there was a possibility of spreading his teaching by peaceful means.

There is a further point of great significance, to which we shall recur later. If Christ renounced warfare he renounced equally definitely all thought of political power and activity. If, therefore, his action is to be taken as a guide, the position of a Prime Minister or a Member of Parliament would be just as un-Christian as that of a general or a soldier. Indeed, it might be argued, with some plausibility, that he regarded the two as mutually connected. 'My kingdom is not of this world. If my kingdom were of this world, then would my servants fight.' This text has been quoted to us many hundreds of times, and the most diverse interpretations given to it. I should personally be inclined to regard it as a simple statement of fact, without any implication of approval or disapproval. But if any further conclusions were to be drawn from it, then the only possible interpretation would seem to be that of some of the small Christian sects who do, in fact, renounce all political activity, namely, that anyone who takes any responsibility for the political ordering of the world may have to be prepared to use armed force.

This does not, however, necessarily affect the main argument of the Christian Pacifist, that war involves, or may involve, participants in it in actions which are incompatible with a true Christian spirit. This is argued persuasively by Dr Cadoux, who quotes, among other instances, some lurid details of instruction in bayonet fighting and some cases of violence to prisoners. He probably exaggerates the extent of such things, but that they do occur is not open to doubt. Their decisiveness as an argument for absolute Pacifism, is, however, much more questionable.

We are discussing the claim of Pacifism as a personal duty. And the convinced Christian, once war has broken out, has to face the personal question of his particular duty in an actual situation, not the general question whether he approves of war or not. And such a question for him would not take the form of asking whether war might have a corrupting effect on people who were not really Christian. If he did try to answer that, he would have to consider, on the lines previously discussed, what the possible alternatives were and what their effects would be. But to decide his personal duty he would have to consider whether he himself could find it possible to maintain a Christian attitude while taking part in a just war, or in a war which was clearly waged against things which he would admit to be extremely evil. He might well feel that it would be extremely difficult. So in different ways would it be in many other activities, for instance, in political party warfare and in many commercial enterprises. It would be extremely hard to take part in running an ordinary business without at times coming to care about making money, a state of mind clearly incompatible with Christ's teaching. Yet is it necessarily impossible in either case? The physical act of killing must, of course, be profoundly repugnant to the Christian, and not to the Christian alone. So, to recur to our earlier example, must be the act of telling a lie, for however good an end. Yet both might equally present themselves, in certain circumstances, as the least evil of possible alternatives.

Apart, however, from the physical act of killing

there is the inner attitude of hatred and violence which seems to be closely bound up with it. And this, it would seem from the teaching recorded in the New Testament, is to be regarded as of much greater significance than the physical action by itself. The Christian, therefore, if he feels that in some cases killing is the only way of preventing something very evil, might well hold that in the mere act of killing by itself he would be blameless if he could keep his soul free of the evil feelings which would generally go with it. There is a phrase attributed to a Spanish Anarchist leader, 'We must learn to kill without hatred'. It sounds, at first hearing, rather grim to us. But is it necessarily un-Christian? That something like it is possible can hardly be denied. We read in the early days of the war of the British officer who swam out into the sea at the risk of his life to rescue a wounded German airman. There must have been some degree of the true Christian attitude here, and there can certainly have been no active hatred. Yet there is no reason to suppose that that officer fought any the less vigorously when the time came to do it. Other similar incidents have been recorded. And, in general, it has several times been remarked that the feeling of hatred in war is usually less noticeable among the actual fighting men than among civilians.*

* I may perhaps be permitted to quote my own experience. In the last war while I was on active service in the army, even in the front line, I was never conscious of any particularly strong feeling of hatred to the enemy. But when I became a prisoner of war and was thus in a position of being forced to follow a policy of non-resistance I found that the discomforts

The whole question of the application of the Christian idea of love to the practical problems of conduct is far more complicated than it apparently seems to many Pacifists. The fact is that a great number of them —this does not, of course, apply to all—have never been faced in their own individual experience with the situations which give rise to these difficulties, and have not enough knowledge or imagination to picture to themselves what they would be like. They have lived relatively sheltered lives in peaceful and law-abiding surroundings, and nothing has happened to them to put any very serious strain on their conviction that they really did love all mankind. I have already referred to the type of conscientious objector, with which we have become quite familiar, who simply ignores or even refuses to believe the accounts of German oppression or cruelty, however well attested. Undoubtedly one motive for this is that he could not help feeling some anger and resentment if the accounts were true, and regarded these feelings as being forbidden by the Christian teaching that he professed.

Yet it would be hard to justify this from the New Testament. However much Christ would have disapproved of resentment at purely personal injuries or settled hatred against an individual he showed by his own behaviour that he would not have regarded anger and indignation against wrongdoing as necessarily evil. When he denounced the Scribes and Pharisees or and petty injustices to which we were from time to time subjected were producing in me an intensity of hatred which, looking back on it, seems altogether out of proportion to the occasions. And I was not alone in this experience.

drove the money-changers from the Temple he was clearly giving expression to these emotions. There was certainly nothing in him of that shrinking from the emotion appropriate to the situation which a one-sided presentation of his teaching would have us adopt. There is nothing in Christ's example to throw doubt on the view that the inability to feel anger is not a virtue but an emotional deficiency.

But the difficulties of interpretation go deeper. As Kant pointed out we cannot feel love to order or by a simple act of will. And the attempt to act as if we could can only too easily lead to insincerity and pretence. I would venture the suggestion that the growth of the doctrine of eternal punishment in the Christian Church may be explained, in part at any rate, as a satisfaction of the feelings of hatred towards the persecutors which the average Christian in the early centuries would not admit that he felt because it seemed to be forbidden by his religion. Another possible result is that to which we have already referred, the refusal to recognise wrongdoing because we are afraid that it might make us angry. There is certainly nothing to excuse that in Christ's own teaching.

If we recognise that love is not something that can be assumed to order or at will, how are we to interpret the emphasis laid on the supreme value of love in the teaching of the New Testament? Clearly it is to be regarded as something good which we should aim at producing both in ourselves and in others, while its opposite, hate, is something bad which we should equally aim at diminishing or destroying. But that does not tell us how we are to pursue this aim in particular circumstances. We cannot do it merely by wishing. Still less can we do it by deceiving ourselves about our own feelings or by running away from or shutting our eyes to the facts in the actual situation which we fear might arouse the wrong emotion in us. Some would doubtless claim that a single religious experience of the nature of conversion would do all that was necessary. There are those of exceptional religious gifts for whom this might be true. But for the ordinary man and woman it is impossible to get away from the need for constant thought, and for constant reconsideration and readjustment of their policy in the light of changing circumstances. And if we recognise this, the Pacifist is faced with the task of proving that his absolute refusal to fight will in all possible circumstances produce more love and less hate in his own mind and in other people than the readiness in certain circumstances to take up arms. And that is just what, if the foregoing argument is correct, he has failed to do.

Most Pacifists, however, seem to read more into it than the mere adoption of the increase of love and the diminution of hate as a general end to be aimed at. They appear to take it as implying an obligation on the individual to act in particular cases as he would do if he already felt perfect love to all human beings, even if they admit that as a fallible and imperfect creature he may not in fact feel always just as he ought to do. But it is not at all clear in many cases how this would lead us to act. It seems to be the assumption of some pacifist arguments that feeling love for another individual would necessitate allowing him freely to commit every sort of crime not only against ourselves but against others as well, if only he is so determined to do so that nothing except force could stop him. That, however, is a very dubious assumption. But at least, the Pacifist would argue, love is absolutely incompatible with killing even a criminal. Even that might be disputed. Anyone who reads the moving account by Hakluyt of Drake's execution of Thomas Doughty must get some inkling of the possibility of the two going together. And I suppose that the Roman father must have felt some love for the sons whom his sense of duty compelled him to put to death for their treason against the State.

That, however, is not the real issue. The chief complication arises from the possibility of conflicting claims between love for one person or set of people and love for another. To most people it would seem that, if they stood by and allowed some dreadful wrong to be done to someone when it was in their power to prevent it by the use of force, they would not be displaying very great love towards the sufferer, whatever they might feel towards the aggressor. The great Christian, David Livingstone, who, if any man ever was, was moved by the purest love and compassion for humanity, recognised the necessity for the use of force, even to the point of killing, to stop slave-raiding in Africa. He had seen its horrors for himself, and was not so obsessed by the duty of loving the slave-raiders as to be complacent towards the sufferings of their victims.* In an instance like this it is particularly clear that, if love for humanity leads one to wish to reduce its sufferings to a minimum, far less suffering would be caused by fighting the slave-raiders than by leaving them to carry on their work unchecked.

The fact is that love is an ambiguous word which can be used to cover several different states of mind. There is the warm personal affection that we feel for particular individuals as individuals. It is obviously only possible to feel this towards people whom we know personally, and we naturally feel it in greater degree for some people than others. This is doubtless a desirable feeling to have. The Christian would have to recognise that Christ himself experienced it. His feeling towards 'the disciple whom Jesus loved' can hardly have been precisely the same as his feeling towards the Scribes and Pharisees whom he denounced. But such a feeling would certainly not be a safe guide to follow in all our actions.

The love of humanity, which is, I suppose, the chief Christian virtue, is something different. It is not a thing which an imperfect human being is capable of feeling all the time. Indeed, an active feeling of love at any one time for all the individuals who com-

---

* Livingstone's life is particularly worthy of study in this connection. Here was a man who faced dangers and suffering, such as most of our Pacifists have never known, for the love of humanity, and yet, not only did he countenance the use of force against slave-raiders, but he did not hesitate to use lethal weapons to protect himself and his party, when attacked. I think that a study of his life ought to make those who claim that Christian love is incompatible with the use of force think again.

pose the human race is probably an impossibility for a finite being. It must rather be conceived of as a settled disposition which will express itself in an active feeling to all human beings alike when the occasion for it arises. It is that in us which is at work, for instance, when we see or hear of the suffering of some individual, whom we do not know personally, and our sympathy and compassion and desire to help are aroused simply and solely because he is a human being. That may well be the supreme virtue. Yet even so by itself it may be a dangerous guide to action unless it is informed by intelligence and imagination, and even with the greatest amount of these it can never be a certain guide. By its own logic it requires us to feel the same to every human being. Yet our human limitations make this impossible as an active feeling. We can only strive to produce such a state of mind in ourselves that, in any given situation, we feel to the individuals whom our actions may affect as we should feel to anyone else in the same situation, and that we act accordingly. But it is often an extraordinarily difficult thing to say what that implies in practice in any particular case.

There are simple cases in which it involves relatively little difficulty. If we see an injured man by the road-side we know that love for humanity would require us to go to his help, whoever he was. And some Pacifists talk as if there was never any more in it than that, a direct relation between two individuals in which it is easy to ask, 'Am I behaving to him as I should like him to behave to me?' So, when it is a question of fighting, and perhaps killing, a German soldier, he knows that he would not like the German soldier to kill him and thinks that settles the matter. But when our choice of action has public reference, when it is a question of co-operating or refusing to co-operate with other people, when our acting or refusing to act is going, to however small a degree, to affect a large number of others, then the question becomes very much more complicated, and admits of no such simple solution. We can say at least that love could not be a merely negative influence which bade us refrain from actions because they might be painful to some people, German soldiers or slave-raiders for instance. It would also lead us to wish to do something positive for the relief of their victims. Nor would it be content with the individual actions which were immediately within our power towards people with whom we were in direct contact at the moment. It would also lead us to work in co-operation with other people to alter a general state of things, the system or institution which made certain evils possible or prevented certain goods. It would be a very one-sided form of love which led a man to labour, however devotedly, to alleviate the lot of individual slaves and yet to do nothing to bring slavery as an institution to an end. And in doing that it might lead him to actions which, purely from the point of view of relations between one individual and another, might seem ruthless. Complete love and complete knowledge would get the right balance between these different considerations. Imperfect human beings can only make the best shot at it that is possible to them in the circumstances. Only they must not ignore any of these considerations or deliberately limit their view to one set alone.

The upshot of this is that the appeal to the principle of love is very far from providing the simple solution to practical problems that many Pacifists seem to suppose. On the contrary, if fairly considered, it will be seen to raise problems rather than to solve them. They cannot, indeed, be solved without taking many other considerations into account, among them all those which have been set out in the foregoing pages.

There are two other doctrines associated with Christianity which have been, or might be, supposed to bear on this question. The doctrine of the Father-hood of God, with its corollary that all men, as His children, have an equal value, though it has been quoted in this connection, does not seem to lead to any decisive conclusions on this particular question. Indeed, some of the considerations put forward in discussing the application of the principle of love would apply equally here. The doctrine would, I suppose, be incompatible with any approval of a war initiated for narrowly nationalistic aims, to put one nation, for instance, in a privileged position as against another. It is difficult to see how it would be incompatible with a war of defence of one nation against another's attempt to ruin or enslave it, even if only these two nations were involved. And in the present instance when almost the whole human race is involved and the issue at stake is the maintenance or destruction of certain values which have no special connection with one country rather than another, it does not seem to have any special bearing at all.

Another doctrine which might be thought to be relevant to the question is the immortality of the soul. Yet in fact, though the great majority of applicants to the Tribunal were members of religious bodies which believe in this doctrine, we hardly ever heard it put forward as a fact which has a bearing on the issue of Pacifism. The only form in which we were familiar with it was in the assertion of the adherents of some of the smaller religious bodies that they could not take the responsibility of killing a man in battle because they might be sending the soul of a sinner to eternal torment without giving him a chance to repent. Yet, apart from that, one would have expected it to be put forward as a relevant consideration. It might have been used to turn the edge of the argument against Pacifism based on considerations of the evil effects in this world of submission to some forms of aggression. It might be argued that what happened in the short span of this life would be of small importance as compared with eternity. Yet perhaps this would be a two-edged weapon. For so many of the arguments for Pacifism are based on just the same grounds, the evil effects of war in this world. Further, the emphasis that some Pacifists seem to lay on the preservation of human life as the supreme good, irrespective of the quality of the life which others would regard as the condition of its being worth preserving, might be seriously weakened by a belief in immortality. Bodily death can hardly be the supreme and final evil if the personality still survives. But it would, of course, make a good deal of difference in what form we pictured the life after death. However, in fact Pacifists do not make much use of this doctrine.

The upshot of this discussion is that, so far as we take the teaching of the New Testament as unfolding an ideal and a spirit in which we should act, while leaving the responsibility to us of how we should apply this to our own varied and ever-changing circumstances, it is impossible to extract from it any injunction to absolute Pacifism and non-resistance. That peace is good and that we should seek to establish it throughout the world is certainly implied in it. But there is no warrant for regarding peace as so supreme over all other goods that we can say that everything else should be sacrificed to it and that nothing can be worse than war.

The situation is rather different if we look to the New Testament to provide us with concrete rules of conduct, absolutely binding on us irrespective of time, place, or circumstances. Even from this point of view there is no decisive and explicit pronouncement on the subject of participation in war. But there is a much stronger case for regarding this as forbidden by impli-cation, particularly if we take the Epistles of St Paul as just as authoritative as the Gospels. The same prin-ciples of interpretation, however, would compel us to renounce a great deal more than merely participation in war. There would certainly be quite as strong a case for saying that the pursuit of wealth, and possibly even the personal possession of it, must be regarded as forbidden. So must participation in public affairs or the assumption of political or legal responsibilities. In fact, if we are to obey in detail the injunctions that were given to the first Christians, we must put ourselves in the same position as the first Christians, and regard ourselves as a small band of believers, living in a world that as a whole has not accepted Christ, following the path of separation and taking no responsibility for the affairs of this world. Our Pacifism, then, will be merely incidental to a much wider renunciation of privileges and responsibilities. This is the line actually followed by some of the smaller Christian sects, such as the Christadelphians and the Plymouth Brethren, and in a rather different form by religious communities like the Huterian Brothers. One cannot but respect their sincerity and consistency. Personally, I feel little doubt that their attitude is much closer to the attitude of the earliest Christians than that of the larger religious bodies. But there is another side to it, and the austerity with which they leave the rest of the world to its fate will repel some of us more than their undoubted virtues will attract. In any case, their fundamental assumption, that what Christ and St Paul laid down for the conduct of the first believers must necessarily have been intended by them to hold for believers in later ages and in very different circumstances, is just what is open to question.

Chapter IV

ALTERNATIVE SERVICE

If, for any of the reasons discussed above, the Pacifist feels that he cannot take an active part in war-like activities, what can he do when his country is actually at war? This is a question which, as a rule, does not receive much attention in the general discussions of Pacifism. Yet it is obviously of vital practical importance, and on the Tribunal by far the greater part of our time was taken up by its consideration. It is a point of special interest in that, to a peculiar degree, it provides a criterion of the sense of logic of the objector and the degree to which he has thought out clearly the implications of his own general position. And, partly for that reason, it reveals the fundamental differences that in reality separate one type of conscientious objector from another.

There is a regrettable tendency towards a sort of unholy alliance between the extreme Pacifists and their extreme critics in an attempt to prove that there is no 'logical' stopping-place between full participation in all war-like activities and absolute refusal to perform any useful service of any kind to a country at war. The critics of Pacifism use this argument to prove that, if an objector is willing to do anything at all, he might as well fight, while the extreme objectors draw from it the conclusion that if they are exempted as genuine objectors from actual fighting they should not be expected to undertake any service for the country at all. But all such arguments display a complete ignorance of what logic is. What logic requires of us is that, if we lay down a general principle, we should apply it consistently to all particular cases of the same kind. But the cases to which it applies depend, of course, on the nature of the general principle. Thus, a conscientious objector who wishes to think logically must think out clearly for himself what exactly are the characteristics of war-like action which he considers make it wrong for him to take part in it. As we have seen, many different answers would be given to this by different types of objector. He must then ask himself whether the same characteristics are found in other kinds of activity which he may be invited to undertake. If they are not, then he has no logical reason for refusing to undertake them.

Let us take the position which has seemed, according to the foregoing argument, the strongest ground for the Pacifist. That is the argument that violent and aggressive action, culminating in actual killing, is incompatible with a Christian attitude towards other human beings. As we have seen, there is a sense in which this is clearly true, and if we could abstract the acts of violence from their wider consequences and implications they would have to be condemned. The non-pacifist, of course, denies the legitimacy of this abstraction. But he ought to be able to understand how the Pacifist comes to feel as he does about it. The question before us now, however, is what actions this extends to. Obviously it includes all specific actions directly aimed at the death or injury of the enemy, such as firing a gun or rifle or using a bayonet. Almost as obviously does it include actions directly intended to assist the first class of actions, such as passing the ammunition for others to fire. And that, it seems clear, must be extended to making the munitions. For those who make them know for what they are intended and must be regarded as willing the use to which they are put. If the wrongdoing consists in feeling towards the enemy in a way which makes you glad of, or unmoved by, his death, then the munition maker is just as much implicated in it as the soldier. It follows that no conscientious objector, whose objection is accepted as genuine, ought to be required to work at making munitions of war. We can, indeed, go further and say that if an objector was willing to work in a munitions factory it would cast grave doubts on the genuineness of his objection.

The case is entirely different, as many of the more sensible objectors see, when it comes to activities directed towards satisfying the common human needs, even of a soldier, such as food or clothing or medical attention when sick or wounded. It is entirely beside the point to argue, as some Pacifists and some of their critics alike do, that these activities are just as important for carrying on the war as the provision of munitions. That could not be the concern of the Pacifist, so far as he takes his stand on the ground we are now considering. If he is a genuine believer in the rights of conscience, he must recognise the right of the soldier to act according to his conscience and take the responsibility for it. While, therefore, he would no doubt be glad to convert the soldier to a genuine belief in Pacifism, he could have no interest in stopping the soldier from fighting by starving him or leaving him to die when wounded. It would, indeed, be both illogical and un-Christian to do so. For the central point of this position lies in its insistence on the need for acting to others, even sinners, in a spirit of love and charity. And this means not merely abstention from violence, but a positive wish to help others, to feed the hungry, for instance, and succour the wounded. It would, indeed, be inconsistent if the need to feel thus was regarded as applying only to the enemy and not to our own people. The Christian who did feel thus would surely welcome the opportunity of undertaking some work aimed at relieving or preventing suffering, and he would welcome it no whit less if it was applied to our own soldiers than he would if it was applied to anyone else. The conscientious objectors who feel most deeply and think most clearly in fact take this view.

To those who still feel doubts about the logic of this distinction one may reasonably call in evidence the practice of the law, which in its very nature represents the attempt to apply general principles consistently to particular cases, in other words, to be logical. If I construct instruments for burglary or forgery, and deliver them to the burglar or forger, knowing the use to which they are going to be put, I shall be regarded as an accessory to their crimes and condemned accordingly. But if I am, let us say, a doctor in a hospital and an injured burglar comes in for treatment, I am not only allowed but am under an obligation to give him the best medical treatment possible. No one in his senses would accuse me of being an accessory to his crimes, even though I might know well that he would resume his burgling as soon as he was cured. Anyone who did argue in that way would really have to say that no doctor should ever treat a sick or injured man unless he was perfectly satisfied that all the patient's subsequent conduct would be beyond reproach. Indeed, if there was to be any analogy to the position of the conscientious objector, we should have to go further and say that the doctor should never treat a patient unless he was satisfied that the patient's conscientious opinion would always agree with his own about what actions were right and what were wrong. For none but the most pharisaical conscientious objector could really regard the position of the burglar as analogous to that of the soldier. That makes the case even stronger.

The distinction between satisfying the ordinary human needs of the fighting man and directly aiding him in the work of fighting is, then, perfectly clear. But there are doubtless certain border-line cases in which the sensitive conscience might feel difficulties. It might, for instance, be a question of transporting food to the soldiers while they were actually fighting, or manufacturing some article which might be or actually was used both for peaceful and for war-like purposes. Such cases, however, are confined within very narrow limits. And the earlier arguments in this discussion have been written in vain if it has not been made clear that the existence of border-line cases casts no sort of doubt at all on the reality of the differences between the great bulk of the cases which are quite clearly on one side or the other of the border, any more than the existence of a temperate zone means that there is no difference between the climate of the North Pole and that of the Equator. The border-line case is, indeed, the happy hunting-ground of sham logic. Genuine logic has no need to ignore the obvious fact that between many, perhaps most, defined classes of objects there is a debatable no-man's land. And if, for practical purposes, a line has to be drawn across it, it necessarily seems arbitrary if we only look at the cases which fall immediately to one side or other of it. So we need not be troubled about our general principle by this very small class of doubtful cases. In practice they can be left to the intuition of the person whose action is in question. A conscientious objector who has, as many of them have, a sound grasp of this general principle of distinction may safely be left to draw the exact line for himself.

We should be all the readier to accept that, because there is a large class of cases in which, from this general point of view, no possible doubt can arise. That is, all the many valuable services that can be performed not only for the soldiers but for the civilian population. Work on the land in order to grow food, work in the fire service or civil defence services, work in civilian hospitals—all these, and others like them, are services which are not only compatible with but seem to be positively enjoined by the Christian teaching of love for humanity as the guiding principle of action. Anyone genuinely moved by this feeling would welcome the opportunity of performing services such as these to suffering humanity. Many, possibly the majority of conscientious objectors in fact do so, and they have at times shown great devotion, and even heroism, in carrying out such duties.

But there are many others who refuse to undertake some or any of such tasks. And the kind of reasons they give for this attitude demand consideration. They reveal clearly the sharp differences that exist between one kind of Pacifist and another in their underlying points of view. The type of conscientious objector of which we have just been speaking is single-mindedly anxious to decide what sort of action a Christian love of humanity would lead to in the circumstances actually obtaining at the time. Of the possible forms of service proposed to him he asks the simple question, Would a love of humanity lead me to desire this to be done in these circumstances? He and an enlightened non-pacifist will differ in particular cases about the answer they would give. But they both understand the question, and can co-operate with mutual satisfaction in those activities in which they both agree about the answer. When, however, we consider the arguments put forward by the type of Pacifist who refuses to participate in these activities we shall find that there is always some other consideration than is raised in this question coming in. Indeed, in some of the arguments used it is difficult to find much trace of the love of humanity at all. For many Pacifists of this type the non-pacifist will find it difficult to feel any respect.

What are the arguments put forward to justify the refusal to undertake some or all of these services? They are very various in themselves. We need not linger over some of the occasional eccentricities with which we have met, such as the view of a very small religious body that they must not join the fire service because they might be required to put out fires in churches or chapels of other denominations, or the view expressed by a member of a Tolstoyan community that he would not put out a fire caused by enemy action in his own house or anyone else's because that was forbidden by the scriptural command, 'Resist not evil'. No rational argument is possible in these cases, which are fortunately rare. But the great majority of objectors to civilian service do attempt to base their objection on some sort of general principle, though by no means always the same one, and these, up to a point, can be rationally discussed.

One ground of objection sometimes put forward to undertaking such services is that it would release a man for military service. There are three things to be said about this argument. In the first place, it is not true, except, perhaps, in rare individual cases. The supply of man-power is not organised so closely that for each individual who goes on the land or enters the fire service another individual is automatically released for the fighting services. In any case, as a general rule the needs of the fighting services come first, so that the only result of a conscientious objector refusing to undertake the duties open to him would be that a little less corn was grown or a little more damage was done by fire, not that there were fewer soldiers or sailors or airmen. Secondly, if man-power really were or could be organised so closely as this, the objection would have to apply not only to undertaking these particular services but to doing almost anything at all. For instance, if the objector was running a shop and was allowed to continue doing so, it might well mean that another shop might be closed down without depriving the public of essential shopping facilities. This seems to be one of the cases in which genuine logic would require the objector on such grounds to go out of the world altogether, unless he was the fortunate possessor of private means.

But the third criticism is more fundamental. We may well ask what pacifist principle requires a conscientious objector to regard it as a duty to try to prevent people, who are not Pacifists, from going into the armed forces. If it were a question of converting them to Pacifism that might be another matter. But that does not arise here. In this case it is a question of keeping them out by putting pressure on them, negative pressure, it is true, in the sense of refusing to render services which it is in his power to render, but that is none the less a real kind of pressure. What the objector is, in effect, saying is, 'If you go into the army, as far as my action affects it, your homes may burn or the country become short of food. So you had better stay at home.' This seems very like an attempt to impose his own view of what is right, not by persuasion but by force. And what good, from his own point of view, does the Pacifist suppose that he is doing by keeping a few men out of the armed forces? He is certainly not diminishing the evils of war. In fact, as we have already seen in another connection, a likely effect of his action, if it had any effect at all, would be to prolong the war. On the other side, it is clear that the services the objector is being asked to perform are such that anyone with any humane feeling would agree ought to be performed. And if this humane feeling was his strongest motive he would want to perform them whatever incidental results might arise. At any rate, the objector who puts forward such grounds as these might quite fairly be asked the question, whether he really believes that the evil of a few more non-pacifists being actually in the armed forces is greater than the evil of a few more homes being destroyed by fire or a few more people being short of food. If he does believe so then it is quite impossible for him to claim that love of humanity is his guiding motive.

Somewhat similar considerations apply to the much more frequent form of objection to taking part in certain activities, for instance, the civil defence services, because they are 'part of the war effort'. There can be no possible doubt that this phrase has become, for many Pacifists, simply a catch-phrase with no thought behind it at all. It is interpreted in practice in a stricter, and a more moderate form. In the former, it is taken, apparently, to forbid participation in any activity which could be of any value to a country at war. 'I will not grow food because it might help to win the war', as one objector said. In the other a distinction is made between activities, such as growing food, which are needed just as much in peace as in war and are, therefore, allowable, and those such as the civil defence or fire services which are only needed because of the war, and are therefore wrong. The latter, no doubt, displays a more amiable frame of mind than the former, but it is no more logical, and both forms are open to the same criticisms.

What is it about a 'part of the war effort' such as the fire service that makes it wrong for a Pacifist to participate in it? It is certainly not because of the grounds for conscientious objection to military service that we have been considering so far, that it might involve one in activities which are incompatible with a true Christian spirit. On the contrary, nothing could be more obviously an expression of Christian love for humanity than an effort to save the lives and homes of the civilian population, and no sort of violence or aggressiveness to anyone is involved in it. Indeed, it is hard to see how a Christian spirit could allow a man to stand by and see these things threatened without an effort to save them. Some objectors have explained that they would help to put out a fire or save a life if they happened to be there at the time, but that they object to joining any organised effort to this end. But this is really the most futile inconsistency. The question they have no right to shirk is whether they think these things ought to be done or not. If they think that they ought to be done then there can be no possible wrong in organising for the purpose. It is absurd to suggest that it can be right to do a thing sporadically and inefficiently but wrong to do it systematically and efficiently, or right to do it as an individual in isolation but wrong to co-operate with others for the purpose. Yet that is what that distinction really comes to.

But the answer that this type of objector would give to the question why he objected to participating in the 'war effort' to this extent would probably take the form of the simple statement that war is wrong. We are back, therefore, to the old objection to war as a policy. We have already discussed the confusions of thought that were evident in the passage from the proposition that no nation should ever go to war to the proposition that no individual, who believed this, ought to participate in war once it had broken out. And if a confusion of thought was established there it is more obviously to be found when the argument is applied to civilian services.

If this type of objector were asked why war was wrong he would, presumably, reply by pointing out all the evils that were involved in it, most notably the suffering that it brought to humanity. Most people would feel that, if they saw suffering going on and were not in a position to stop it altogether, they would at least wish to reduce the amount as far as lay in their power. And anyone who joined, say, the fire service or a first-aid party would be doing something in this direction. The objector who refuses to take part in such services is really saying that, as far as he is concerned, if he cannot stop the suffering altogether he is content for it to remain at the maximum and does not wish it to be reduced in amount. It is in vain for him to attempt to shirk his own responsibility in the matter by throwing the blame on the Government. He may say, as the Duke of Bedford said in the House of Lords in defending the refusal of certain objectors to take part in fire duties, that if the Government does not want the people's homes to burn, they ought to make peace. But what the Government does is not his responsibility or under his control. The question he ought to ask himself is whether *he* wants the people's homes to burn. He is not being asked to help to save them from burning as a favour to the Government, but because it is presumed that, even if he cannot save them altogether, he would prefer that as many should be saved as possible. If he really would not prefer that, if he prefers to take the line, 'If they can't be saved in my way, let them burn', then whatever case he may put up for his attitude, he certainly cannot pretend that it is based on love for humanity or compassion for its sufferings.

Those of us who have listened to considerable numbers of these extreme objectors expounding their views will find it hard not to believe that in some cases part, at any rate, of the motive for their attitude is a personal resentment against a society which has rejected their views. I would not, however, suggest that this would apply to the majority of such cases. What seems to be more often at work is an irrational association of ideas. They begin by experiencing an emotional revulsion against war because of the sufferings it brings. That is, of course, perfectly intelligible. But they go on to transfer this feeling to other activities which are associated with war, even though the reason for their revulsion from war does not apply to these activities at all. It is rather like a form of the conditioned reflexes with which Pavlov's experiments have made us familiar. It is, perhaps, still closer to some of the forms of neurosis with which the psycho-analysts deal, where a phobia or some other violent emotional reaction is developed for some apparently harmless object, because, in one way or another, it has become associated in the unconscious mind of the patient with something quite different.

In some cases we found this carried to most eccentric lengths. One applicant not only objected to having a gas-mask—'the Devil's implement', as he called it—for himself, but also refused to allow his wife or child to have one. Another pointed with pride to the fact that, when paying his rates, he had deducted the amount that was stated on the demand note to be devoted to A.R.P. services. But all these extreme objectors, if they did not go as far as this, displayed the same inability to judge of a concrete act in an actual situation. They preferred to take refuge in vague, abstract phrases such as 'the war effort', oblivious of the fact that this is a blanket term covering a variety of activities, some of which, no doubt, involve an intensification of the sufferings caused by war, while others can have no possible effect of that kind, but instead are directed to mitigating those sufferings. The reasons for disapproving of the former are necessarily, to anyone who thinks rationally, reasons for approving of the latter. And the feelings that led anyone to shrink from the former would equally lead him to welcome the latter, unless they were distorted by unrecognised psychological processes such as those described.

There are various other forms of objection to this or that particular service, characteristic of certain small religious groups, which can only be mentioned briefly or not at all. Some members of those groups which aim at modelling the life of their own community on the pattern of the early Christians feel that their desire to 'walk in the path of separation' is infringed by membership of any organised body under the Government or concerned with the affairs of the State, particularly when it exercises coercive powers. In the same way, in peace-time they refuse to join Trade Unions or political parties, or, in some cases, any branch of Government service. On their own premises there is undoubtedly much to be said for this attitude. Those who do not accept the basic assumptions of their interpretation of Christian teaching can hardly argue the point with them without attacking these basic assumptions. We can only note with satisfaction that for a considerable number of them their anxiety to be of help to the community has overcome any scruples they might feel about enlisting in these services.

There still remains for consideration the position of that small minority of Pacifists whose fundamental objection is to any form of compulsion. These are chiefly to be found among the more extreme members of the Society of Friends, but a few have appeared in other quarters. It has not been easy to find any coherent moral principle at the back of this view, and, even in so small a group as this, considerable variations were to be found in the way in which it was presented.

One presentation of the view claimed that a government has no right to introduce compulsion for military purposes, even for people who have no moral objection to military service and no moral objection to compulsion. A small number of those who took this line refused even to register as conscientious objectors. It is very hard to find any rational argument in support of this view. It is not a question of a government having no right to order people to do what they think wrong; that is already recognised by the provision made for conscientious objection. The claim is, rather, that a government has no right to order people to do what they think right, if the conscientious objector thinks it wrong. It is, in fact, a claim that the Government—and that must include all the people who support the Government—ought to be guided, not by their own consciences, but by the conscience of the objector. This is a curious position for the defenders of the rights of conscience to adopt; and it must be admitted that they do not often realise the implications of their own view. There is possibly a confusion in the meaning attached to 'having a right' to do anything. Of course, there is a general sense in which no one, government or individual, 'has a right' to do wrong, even if they think it right. In that sense, the Pacifist necessarily believes that no State 'has a right' to declare war at all. If they had a right to declare war, it could hardly be maintained that they had no right to use such compulsion as they thought necessary, unless, indeed, it was maintained that all compulsion for any end, good or bad, was wrong. We shall have a word to say about that position later. But for the moment we are concerned with the view that compulsion is specially wrong for the purposes of war. And from that point of view it would appear that it was the war rather than the compulsion in which the wrong lay.

There is, however, another sense in which we use the phrase 'having a right' to do anything in a more restricted application. That is when we recognise the relative justification for action that we personally think wrong when it is taken by another person who sincerely believes that it is right. That is the basis of toleration. It is the principle to which the conscientious objector appeals, and which he ought to be particularly ready to extend to other people. Yet in adopting the attitude now under discussion it is clear that he is denying it. He is not, indeed, forcibly repressing the view of which he disapproves. He is hardly in a position to do so. But he states that he refuses to 'recognise' or to 'acknowledge' an Act of Parliament even though it does not require him to do anything which he thinks wrong. And that, if it is anything more than a futile gesture of irritation, amounts to denying even a relative justification for those responsible for this policy, which includes, as we have seen, to some degree, the great majority of the electorate, taking action which they believe to be right. There could hardly be a more glaring instance of self-contradiction.

A similar process of thought is, presumably, at the back of the minds of those, again very few, who say that they will perform certain services but not 'as a condition of exemption from military service' or that they will not 'bargain with the authorities' for exemption. This is obviously a mere verbal quibble, which does not express any distinctions in reality. There is nothing that can really be described as bargaining. And as for the question whether it is regarded as a condition of exemption or not, that is not really in the power of the objector to decide, but depends on the way in which it is regarded by the authorities who decide about the exemption. They exempt a man from military service because they believe he has a conscientious objection to it. What further order they will make depends on the circumstances. Occasionally we have had applicants who objected to accepting any condition but assured us that, if they were exempted unconditionally, they would continue doing some valuable kind of work which they were already doing. When we were completely satisfied that this was so, we have sometimes given them what they asked, because we have accepted their assurance. In reality, in doing this we have accepted a condition for unconditional exemption. At a certain University where students who objected to joining the Senior Training Corps were required to perform special fire guard duties, a student stated to the authorities that he was quite willing to perform these duties voluntarily—he was, in fact, already doing so—but objected to doing so under compulsion. The Vice-Chancellor replied, soothingly, 'All right! As long as you perform them voluntarily we shan't ask anything more of you.' The student went away quite satisfied, and continued in the punctilious performance of his duties.

The matter is approached from a somewhat different angle by those who claim an unconditional right for each man to choose his work in the world for himself. To quote a statement by one objector who took this point of view, 'The restriction involves a denial to the individual of freedom to choose his work in accordance with the dictates of his conscience and prevents him from changing his occupation if he feels called upon to do so. This freedom is a basic moral right and one of the things for which the country is fighting.' Pronouncements on the same lines have been made by other objectors from time to time.

In fact, there is no such absolute or 'basic' moral right, and could not possibly be so. Of course, as most people would agree, it is a good thing that as many people as possible should be able to choose the occupation that suits them, and in the society which we should like to build after the war we should hope to make this possible for a great many more people than it has been previously, even in peace-time. In that sense, we might describe this as one of the things that we are fighting for. But that is a very different thing from claiming it as an absolute and unconditional right. It cannot be such an unconditional right, because, as a matter of fact and, most people would say, as a matter of right, too, it has to be balanced against other considerations, particularly the 'right' of the rest of the community to have the services they require. This latter right is enforced most obviously by the working of economic demand. It is no use feeling the call to produce a certain kind of goods or do a certain kind of service if no one wants them enough to pay for them.* And, once we recognise that, it is impossible to argue that it would be immoral for this demand, under certain circumstances and particularly in times of emergency, to be formulated consciously by the community through its recognised organs of government.

There are, of course, other ways in which the 'individual's freedom to choose his work' is rightly restricted. No one, for instance, can practise as a doctor, however much he feels that that is his proper vocation, unless he can pass his examinations, or become a clergyman unless he can find a Bishop to ordain him. But these are minor illustrations of the general principle that other people, beside the man himself, are concerned in the work he proposes to do. It is really a sign of a hypertrophied sense of his own importance for a man to claim to be the sole judge of the services that he should render to the community, leaving the community no voice in the matter at all. Properly, even in an ideal State, both sides should have some say, and the final decision should be a matter of

---

* For instance, we have seen members of Jehovah's Witnesses who had felt the call to become whole-time evangelists, but had had to abandon it because they could not earn a living at it. In what sense had they a 'right' to adopt this vocation?

mutual adjustment and agreement. And that is, in fact, how the Conscientious Objector Tribunals, or at any rate the great majority of them, work. They consult with the applicant about the kind of work that he feels drawn to, and formulate their conditions in general terms, leaving the applicant a considerable range of freedom of choice. The great majority of objectors, fortunately, are reasonable enough to recognise this and are glad to co-operate with the Tribunals and come half-way to meet them.

There remains the view, which we met with a few times and heard of more frequently, that all compulsion is wrong and should be resisted, whatever its purpose. This principle we heard stated in set terms. But it was not always easy to extract from the applicants exactly how far they really believed that it should be applied. One of them did, indeed, state that if he had a car he would regard it as wrong to drive on the side of the road prescribed by the law. We put, once or twice, what seemed to us a relevant instance by asking whether they would refuse to have their children educated, because education was compulsory, but failed to extract a decisive answer. They certainly did not repudiate this application of their views. We were particularly struck by the cases in which an objector was already doing, of his own choice, some valuable piece of work but stated that, if the Tribunal made an order that he should continue in this occupation, he would feel bound to give it up. We were informed of several other cases elsewhere in which this attitude had been adopted.

It is very difficult to think of any rational justification for this point of view, nor did we receive much help in this from those who put it forward. 'I must be free' was the usual cry, which seemed to us to imply a conception of 'freedom' which excluded all co-operation with others, for co-operation is clearly impossible if we are never prepared to modify or withdraw our view in order to come to an agreement with other people. It seemed, indeed, only possible in a world which contained no other human beings. The nearest approach to a rational argument that we heard was the statement that an act had no moral value if done in obedience to an order from someone else. There is, however, a confusion of thought here. It is doubtless true that if an action is done *merely* because it is ordered under threat of punishment, it has no positive moral value. But that does not mean that it becomes bad. If I refrain from committing a murder merely because I am afraid of being hanged I can claim no credit for that, but that does not mean, in any sense, that it was a bad thing not to commit the murder. However, that is not in question here. If, on the other hand, I welcome and approve of a particular course of action, if I should have chosen it whether it were ordered or not, and still more if I have already chosen it before it was ordered, the moral value of the action is in no way diminished if it is ordered. If, for instance, I work in a hospital to relieve suffering, the moral value of my action lies in my feeling of love and compassion and sense of obligation towards suffering humanity. And this, if it is genuinely felt, is not in any way diminished by my being ordered to do what I should have done anyhow.

If, on the other hand, I refuse to do this work merely because it is ordered, that can only mean that my desire to relieve suffering is not so strong as my sense of personal dignity, or whatever is infringed by the fact of being ordered to do anything. And that is not an admirable state of mind. To anyone who, without thinking of himself, is single-mindedly anxious that a piece of work should be done, the question whether he has been ordered to do it or not will seem quite irrelevant. This revulsion from the idea of doing anything just because it has been ordered, irrespective of its merits, can really only be understood on psychological grounds. The most convincing explanation of it is that it arises from an unacknowledged sense of some weakness of personality which makes a man frightened of being under orders because he does not feel strong enough to stand up to it and still remain himself.

Before leaving this subject, it is necessary to insist that this idea that there is something essentially evil about obeying orders finds no support of any kind in the teaching of Christ and his immediate followers as recorded in the New Testament. St Paul's statements, in particular, are quite unequivocal in their repeated emphasis on the duty of obeying the commands of the lawful authority as long as what they command is not positively wrong in itself. But Christ's own statements, though less frequent, are quite as explicit. In particular we may note the text 'Whosoever shall compel thee to go a mile, go with him twain'. Dr Cadoux interprets this as referring to the practice of the Roman authorities of using forced labour for the construction of roads. If that is correct, it is particularly apposite to the present question, as these roads were intended largely for the movement of troops. But, in any case, it is clear that the authentic Christian teaching is that orders given by a lawful authority, if they do not command anything positively wrong, should not only be obeyed, but obeyed willingly and cheerfully, with a readiness to give even more than is asked for. The religious bodies which base their code of conduct most closely on the words of the New Testament see this clearly.

I have dwelt on the general objection to compulsion at much greater length than the very small numbers of those who maintain it would seem to warrant. This is partly because of the interesting fallacies that it involves, and partly because this small group of objectors has tended to receive an undue amount of publicity. There is a tendency among some writers in the Press, not necessarily themselves Pacifists, to romanticise anyone who defies a government. One writer in the *New Statesman* even declared that this was 'the real ground' for conscientious objection, an assertion which those who have troubled to read these pages will know to be extremely wide of the truth. At any rate, it all helps to bring out the point that I was most concerned to make, namely, the extreme differences in the fundamental moral outlook of the various types of people grouped together under the title of conscientious objector. And these fundamental differences naturally produce equally marked differences in the attitude of the non-pacifist to the different types of conscientious objector. It is with that that we have now to deal.

NOTE ON NON-COMBATANT SERVICE IN THE ARMY

This provided a special problem, though its practical importance was not very great. After the R.A.M.C. ceased to be a strictly non-combatant corps, the only place for those objectors who were assigned to non-combatant service was in the Non-Combatant Corps. Here they were required to do similar work to the Pioneer Corps, and were statutorily protected from having to carry arms and even from having to handle or transport any 'aggressive material'. Roughly about one-fifth of the total number of objectors were willing to accept this.

Their grounds for accepting this were clear. Their objection was to participation in acts of violence, and here they were protected from this. They drew the distinction, already referred to, between affording direct help to such acts (as by transporting munitions), and helping to satisfy the ordinary human needs of those in the combatant forces. As one applicant said, when told that part of their work might be building barracks, 'That's all right! Soldiers have to have somewhere to sleep as much as anyone else.'

The grounds for refusing it, on the part of those who were willing to accept any form of service under civil control, were much less clear. Some objected to the symbolism of wearing a uniform. Others objected specially to being under the orders of army officers, and others, more generally, to being 'part of the military machine'. It is difficult to regard these objections as logically valid. They seem to rest on the kind of irrational association of ideas, which has already been discussed, and to be closely analogous to the wider objection to 'taking part in the war effort'.

On the other hand, it is possible to see how those of particularly delicate conscience could feel that in joining such a corps they might be involved in participation in acts of violence to a degree that could not occur in purely civilian services. They might, for instance, find themselves working on roads which were primarily useful for transport of munitions or passage of armed vehicles. This seems to be one of those border-line cases in which the path of wisdom would be to let the objector decide for himself, whatever we may think of such nice scruples, particularly when other forms of service are open to him in which he would feel quite comfortable. It is possible, also, that some of the more public-spirited objectors really felt that some other form of work would be of greater benefit to humanity, or even to their own country, than membership of this Corps. And here, in many cases, they would undoubtedly be right. No one who has seen the work of the Non-Combatant Corps would put it very high in the ranks of valuable services. It is a great pity that, once a valid objection to combatant service had been established, more latitude was not given to Tribunals or to objectors with regard to this particular choice.

CHAPTER V

SOCIETY AND THE PACIFIST

What attitude should the members of a non-pacifist
society adopt towards Pacifists? How should they feel
and act as individuals towards them, and how would
they wish the community, of which they are members,
to act towards them through its public opinion and its
constituted authorities? It is important to put the
question in this way, because there is a certain tendency
among some Pacifists to talk as if the question at issue
was solely, or mainly, between themselves and an
abstract entity called 'the State'. In reality, it is a
question between them and the vast majority of the
individuals who make up the community. The conscientious objector's position is not only affected by
the legislative or executive action of the Government,
but also by the actions of individuals and the state of
public opinion. Indeed, this last determines, within
narrow limits, what the action of the Government
will be.

It would be an interesting study to attempt an
examination of the actual reactions of the different
elements in public opinion to the conscientious objector. But it would be a task of great magnitude, and
it is doubtful whether the necessary material for it
exists. Certainly no easy or simple generalisations
about it would be possible. For if, as we have seen,
such diversity of opinion and temperament exists
within the relatively small group of Pacifists, we shall

clearly find among the large group of non-pacifists, who may have nothing in common with each other except the negative fact of not being pacifist, the widest possible variety of attitude and outlook. It is easier to attempt some suggestions as to how they ought to react, both as individuals and as members of the State.

It would probably be generally admitted in theory, though much less widely realised in practice, that it is a good thing for the non-pacifist to try to understand the conscientious objector. But that is a complicated and difficult thing. It is relatively easy to examine the arguments that are put forward in explicit terms. It is harder, but still by no means impossible, to discover and analyse the general ideas and assumptions which lie at the back of these arguments. But real understanding of a person involves, also, an examination of the temperamental and emotional factors which make up his character. And this is difficult enough in the case of a single individual whom we know personally. When it comes to generalisations about large numbers, the task seems almost impossible. None the less anyone who comes into contact, in one way or another, with a considerable number of conscientious objectors is bound to form certain impressions. And, if we are careful to make it clear that they are no more than impressions and liable to modification by further knowledge, there is no harm in setting them down. This will be relevant to the present discussion because obviously our own attitude towards objectors will be affected by the psychological factors which we believe to be working in them.

I would record, then, as the first impression, that conscientious objectors differ temperamentally among themselves as widely as they differ intellectually, and that any generalisation about the whole or the great majority of them is certainly false. Thus, in certain circles, one hears language used which suggests that conscientious objectors as a whole are mainly influenced by personal fear of death or injury. A slightly more charitable view goes so far as to admit that this, while it is present, may not be their conscious motive. Yet it would be hard to maintain this in any form about objectors who have, for instance, joined the fire service or volunteered for bomb disposal work. It is only a tentative impression, but I do not myself believe that personal fear plays much part in the decision of more than a very small minority. I have, particularly with some of the more unco-operative objectors, felt a suspicion of various motives at work other than a rational conviction—dislike of being disturbed in their accustomed way of life, dislike of being under discipline and of other features of army life, and the like. But I do not personally believe that the fear motive plays much part.

At the other extreme, the view has been put forward by eminent psychologists that Pacifism is a symptom of repressed Sadism, or more generally of repressed tendencies to violence. Some writers on psychology have even laid down a general law that every strongly felt moral judgement is the result of a repressed tendency in the opposite direction. This may well be so in some cases. Indeed, in a certain type of aggressive and truculent objector with which we became familiar the repression seems to have been very far from complete. But, even here, we shall do well to remember that truculence in the expression of a view may often in reality be a sign of a secret doubt about the conviction that is being expressed. What I have more frequently suspected, however, in a certain type of objector, was a general fear of violent emotion, due either to an abnormally sensitive nervous system or to an imperfectly integrated personality too easily thrown out of balance. But that only applies to a limited number of cases. In general, it seems to me that the different types of conscientious objector that we have seen differ so much from each other that a psychological explanation that would apply to one cannot possibly apply to another.

We must remember, too, in considering all such psychological explanations, the great extent to which opinions are formed, neither by purely rational processes nor by innate emotional tendencies, but by the more accidental factors in our lives, the influence and suggestion of the people with whom we happen to have come into contact, the external conditions in which we happen to have lived, or the particular experiences which happen to have come to us. It has already been pointed out how many Pacifists have had their minds turned in that direction by the influence of their families or by some dominant personality with whom they happen to have come into contact at an impressionable period of their lives. Others have clearly been specially influenced by some event which has brought a particular aspect of the situation home to them. That, indeed, can work both ways. In the first year or two of the war each successive aggression by the enemy brought a crop of conversions from Pacifism on the part of objectors who had previously applied for, or been awarded exemption. These were often among the most obviously sincere applicants. I venture to think that there would have been a great many more withdrawals if applicants could have spent a period in an occupied country under German rule so that they could realise the evils of the alternative as vividly as they realised the evils of war.

If we consider the extreme differences between the contrasted types of conscientious objector, it will be obvious that in many cases there must be an entirely different psychological make-up at the back of them. Consider, on the one hand, the objector who feels that, as one of the best of this type said to us, if he cannot give service by fighting he is under an obligation to give a hundred and fifty per cent service in some other way. He may, perhaps, have thrown up a good job to undertake the most strenuous and dangerous work that was open to him. Contrast with him the opposite type, whose one concern is to keep away from the war and to avoid doing anything that will help in 'the war effort'. He regards it as a virtue to be as unco-operative as he can and refuses to undertake any service that he can possibly avoid, except the work that he is already earning his living by in peace-time. In between these two there is a wide variety of intermediate types, some approximating more to one extreme, some to the other. There are some, too, with special features of their own. For instance, there are those who are anxious to be of service and will make sacrifice to this end, but cannot bring themselves to make the sacrifice of submitting to anyone else's authority. Then there are the religious communities, like the Bruderhof, whose Pacifism is only a part of a much wider renunciation of the things of this world. In all this wide variety of types there must be an equally wide variety of psychological factors at work.

As he comes to understand these differences, the non-pacifist, in his turn, will probably come to feel very differently towards the different types. For those of the first type he will have no reasonable grounds for feeling any dislike or resentment. His disagreement with their views will be quite compatible with a mutual liking and respect. But it would be impossible for him to feel the same towards those of the second type. Their attitude must inevitably seem to him to involve a denial of any obligation to a community which does not accept their views, and even an indifference to what happens to the members of it. And such an attitude, however sincerely held, is not an amiable one, and can hardly excite either respect or liking from those who suffer, to however small a degree, from their denial of their obligations.

There is a further question which arises in this connection. Can there be any intellectual co-operation between the Pacifist and the non-pacifist? Can they take counsel together and arrive at conclusions to which both sides have contributed something? I am afraid that, even with the best type of Pacifist, the answer to this question must be, No. Pacifism, in all its forms, is an all-or-nothing doctrine, which must be accepted entirely or not at all. It implies the assertion of a universal proposition that all war (or, in some forms, all use of force) is wrong. The non-pacifist, on the other hand, does not maintain any contrary universal proposition, that, for instance, all war is right or that the use of force is always justified. He maintains the more modest position that some wars may be right, in the sense that, in some circumstances, war may be the less evil of possible alternatives. That is clearly a stronger position to occupy, as much more evidence is needed to establish an absolutely universal rule, which a single exception would nullify. The result of this is that, in discussions of policy, the non-pacifist is constantly concerned with the question whether the evils of a possible situation are so great that they make it necessary to face the prospect of war as, in those circumstances, a lesser evil. But to the Pacifist this cannot be a real question at all and he can contribute nothing to its solution.

The suggestion, sometimes put forward, that even in a non-pacifist society the Pacifist does contribute something by bearing his testimony against war and thus keeping people's minds constantly alive to its evils, cannot, I think, be maintained. It is absurd to suggest that one cannot be fully alive to the evils of war unless one believes it to be the worst of all possible evils. I believe it to be the case that, in actual fact, much more has been done to rouse the public as a whole from their tendency to accept wars as inevitable by some of the non-pacifist workers for peace than by the Pacifists. Indeed, the advocacy of an extreme position, such as Pacifism, is likely rather to produce a reaction in the opposite direction.

We come, now, to the important question, what policy a non-pacifist State ought to adopt towards Pacifists. Most people only begin to think about this in time of war or when war is clearly imminent. Yet it would obviously be much better if people would think about it and decide their own attitude beforehand, rather than hastily reacting without consideration when the occasion arises. There are some people who, during the war, have adopted a very hostile attitude to all conscientious objectors and expressed the view that they should not be tolerated. Yet those people knew very well that there were religious bodies which included Pacifism as part of their system of belief, and yet they never objected to the toleration of these bodies in time of peace. What right have they, then, to object to the members of these bodies being allowed to act, when war came, as they have always said they were going to act? There would certainly be good grounds for complaint, if, without warning beforehand, the State were suddenly to withdraw the toleration that it had previously extended to them.

What attitude, then, should the State adopt as a settled policy? Should we say that the State must absolutely and unconditionally recognise the right of everyone to act as his conscience bids him in all possible circumstances? It would be hard to justify that as a matter of theory, and quite impossible for a State to apply it in practice if it wished organised society to go on existing. The Indian Thugs were doubtless highly conscientious in the practice of their religion when they murdered innocent travellers by strangling them as a sacrifice to their goddess. Yet how many people would say that the State ought to tolerate such behaviour as this? At any rate, to say that anyone who thought that the Thugs ought to be suppressed was thereby denying all belief in liberty of conscience would be a patent absurdity. No civilised State, indeed, would tolerate a religion which demanded human sacrifice, even if, as has sometimes happened, it could find willing victims from among its adherents.

What we can say is that forcing, or trying to force, people to do anything against their conscience is a bad thing, just as war is a bad thing, only to be justified if it is clearly shown that it is the sole alternative to some other greater evil. There are, however, certain additional complications which have to be borne in mind. When we speak of forcing people to do things, we generally mean inflicting legal punishment on them if they refuse. And if we do not inflict any punishment, we should be generally regarded as exercising toleration towards them. But toleration in the sense of immunity from legal penalties is one thing, and toleration by being put in a privileged position as compared with the rest of the community is another. The conscientious objector who demands unconditional exemption and intends to use it to go on in the same position and occupation as in peace-time is clearly asking for a very special privilege. And here the burden of proof shifts over to his side. The State ought to demand a clear proof that it is to the advantage, not only of the objector but also of the rest of the community, before it allows such a privilege.

Those responsible for the policy of the State will naturally approach the different types of conscientious objector with different feelings, according as they approximate to the co-operative or the unco-operative type. With those of the former type, who are ready to undertake any service other than military to help the community, there could be no possible grounds either of right or expediency for attempting to apply coercion. It would be the height of stupidity to shut a man up in prison who was able and willing to render valuable service at a time when so many kinds of service are badly needed. He can be regarded as a man unfit for military service, only by temperament and conviction instead of by physical incapacity, or alternatively, if we like to put it in more complimentary language, as a man with a special vocation for some kind of service other than military. In any case, he recognises his obligations to the community and the community recognises his value to it, and they can co-operate with mutual satisfaction.

Whether the arrangements actually made for the use of such people was the best possible is more open to question. There can be no doubt that the Government of the time made a creditable effort, not only to recognise conscientious objection but to recognise the different types of conscientious objection and to arrange for them accordingly. No other Government, to the best of my knowledge, has gone to the same lengths. But it is only natural that several years of experience should indicate certain possible improvements, and in what follows a few tentative suggestions will be put forward. Whether the conditions are likely to arise again which will make them of practical value is, of course, open to question. Various questions about national service are undoubtedly likely to arise. But what the probability, if any, is of the recurrence of a situation in which the whole nation has to be organised for the purposes of war is another matter. However, it is mainly to such a situation that the experience gained in the present war would apply. It will be discussed, therefore, on that basis, and, even if the situation never does arise, some of the general conclusions may still have a certain amount of interest.

It seems clear that the primary consideration should be the value of the work to be done. And, in estimating that, the tastes and ability and sense of vocation of the individual should be given due weight, as factors that make for efficiency. It should always be remembered that to put a man at work on a job of first-rate importance which he does indifferently may be, in the total summing-up, of less value to the community than keeping him on at a job of somewhat less importance in itself which he does really well. All these things have to be balanced against each other in deciding where the conscientious objector's services can be best applied for the benefit of the community. And that is the chief consideration in deciding the work to which he is to be assigned.

But, cutting across this, there is another principle which to some of those in authority has seemed also of great importance. That is that the objector should, as far as possible, not be allowed to gain any material advantage by his objection as against the non-objector who enters one of the services. This may often be in contradiction with the first principles. Thus, its requirements are most completely' met by service in the non-combatant corps in the army. But no one could possibly maintain that service in the non-combatant corps was the most valuable service that any conscientious objector could render to the community. Indeed, in the scale of valuable services this particular service would undoubtedly come pretty low. Even when an objection to non-combatant service in the army has been recognised, some Tribunals have felt that at any rate the objector should not be allowed to remain in the position that he was occupying in civilian life, even though this may mean transferring him from valuable work which he was doing well to less valuable work that he would do badly.

The feeling at the back of this must undoubtedly be taken into account. And certainly no conscientious objector could complain of injustice if this principle was applied, nor, to do them justice, would many of this type of objector do so. All the same, it is difficult rationally to defend it. For it may involve a deliberately inefficient allocation of man-power at a time

when the most efficient allocation of it possible is a
vital national interest. At any rate it seems clear that,
if that is to be the policy, it should be decided by the
Government and not left to the feelings of particular
tribunals. On the other hand, it undoubtedly is
desirable that grounds for resentment against conscientious objectors being in a specially favoured position should be removed as far as possible. Some feeling
of hostility among considerable numbers of people
there will inevitably be, but it should be reduced to
the minimum.

The solution would seem to be, if it were adminis-
tratively possible, that all conscientious objectors who
were willing to render service should become for the
duration of the war members of a special organisation
where their financial position would approximate as
nearly as possible to what it would have been in the
services. Something like that appears to have been
attempted in the United States, where every objector
who received exemption was automatically put into a
Civilian Service Corps. Unfortunately, the range of
work open to members of this corps was very limited,
being, in the main, confined to agriculture, forestry,
land reclamation and kindred work. This might often
involve a great waste of special abilities and acquired
knowledge, and the neglect of other fields in which
their services might be equally or more valuable. To
be satisfactory, it would have to be much more flexible
than this, with power to assign them to any kind of
work, including in some cases the work that they were
already doing in civilian life. It would probably also

be desirable to recognise as affiliated bodies certain organisations started by Pacifists themselves, such as the Friends' Ambulance Unit. There would, of course, be many practical difficulties in arranging all this, which could hardly be discussed here. But at least it would meet the requirements of the two principles laid down above.

There remains for consideration the position of the residue of objectors who are completely non-co-operative and refuse to undertake any service that is required by a community at war. Here we are certainly approaching the limits of toleration. The Government declared that they would not recognise a conscientious objection to fire prevention duties, though somewhat illogically they did not apply compulsion to objectors exempted unconditionally. This is a clear case where refusal to take part in these activities goes beyond mere negative inaction and inflicts positive injury on others, by the added burden it throws on them and the increased danger of damage from fire. Nor has any government ever recognised the right to refuse to pay taxes which are raised for the purposes of war, though there would obviously be just as much reason for refusing this as for refusing every other kind of civilian service. Obviously the obligations between an individual and the rest of the community are mutual, and a man who refuses all co-operation with a community has no grounds for complaint if the community refuses to recognise any obligations towards him. This is particularly clear in time of war, when even having enough food to live on involves a great deal of mutual service, including often great danger to individuals. The man who says, 'I will not grow food because it might help to win the war', certainly invites the retort, 'Then why should anyone else grow food, or still more bring it across the sea, for you?' At any rate, it seems difficult to deny the community the right to lay down a minimum degree of co-operation which it will demand from all its members.

How is it, then, to treat those who refuse to fulfil these conditions? The normal way would be to deal out legal penalties just as to any other law-breakers. As we have seen, the fact that their motives are, in some sense, conscientious does not of itself provide a reason why they should be exempt from penalties for breaking the law. But, it may be argued, what is to be gained by putting them in prison? It will not make them carry out the services that we want from them, and it makes them merely a useless expense and burden to the State. The latter point is hardly of much weight, as they are already to a great extent a useless burden. The former is of more weight, but it raises the whole question of the utility of punishment for any breach of the law, and can hardly be discussed without consideration of all the wider repercussions of a condonation of law-breaking.

It must be admitted, however, that imprisonment is not a very imaginative treatment of crime in any circumstances, though in some it would be hard to find an alternative. But in the present case there are certain alternatives which may or may not be practicable, but are at least appropriate to the facts of the situation. To those who refuse to contribute anything that the community requires in an emergency it would be a logical reply for the community to refuse to contribute anything to them. A strict and rigid idea of justice would suggest that the community might renounce its responsibility for supplying them with food by the refusal of a ration book. It might go further and suggest complete outlawry, the refusal of the protection of the law or any other legal rights. But feelings of humanity and considerations of public order alike would probably prevent any State from proceeding to these lengths. In earlier periods of history banishment would have been an appropriate treatment. But that is, in most cases, ruled out by modern conditions, particularly in the case of extreme conscientious objectors who would not be received in any other country with the same degree of toleration that they get here. There remains the possibility of limited deprivation of legal privileges falling short of absolute outlawry. How far this could go would be a matter for legal and administrative discussion, into the details of which it would be inappropriate to enter here.

The general principle remains. Entire refusal to contribute anything to the needs of a community at war no more calls for toleration in the name of liberty of conscience than would attempts at sabotage by a conscientious Fascist. But the community and its government should recognise that this is a regrettable thing, and they should go as far as possible in making it easy for the objector to one form of co-operation to offer another. That is, in fact, substantially the line that this country has taken.

CONCLUSION

Here then, ends the task that I have set before myself in this book. It is an attempt to establish, as against the Pacifist, the propositions that there are certain evils which are worse than war and that there are circumstances in which these can only be met by fighting. And it is also argued that there can be no rational moral principle which requires an individual in all circumstances to refuse to participate in a war once it has been started, even if he disapproved of it in the first place. I have discussed these positions as if they were matters for rational argument and evidence. Indeed, there is no other way in which they can be discussed. Yet I know well that argument and evidence can never, by themselves, play the decisive part in moral decisions. Quite apart from individual irrationalities, it is true for everyone that moral beliefs can never be a reality unless they are felt as well as proved. And what we feel cannot be decided for us by a single chain of arguments. Yet in the long run even what we feel is affected by how we think, so that an attempt at rational argument is never entirely waste of time.

Further, the non-pacifist can never afford to forget that, when he has rejected the simple solution of the Pacifist, he is only at the beginning of his own problems. For he has to decide for himself what kind of evils he regards as so bad that they must be met by fighting, if that is the only way. That is not, perhaps, such a difficult task in the present circumstances, because nearly everyone, including most Pacifists, would agree that if there ever was an evil that was worse than war it would be the establishment of a regime such as that of Hitler and the Nazi government of Germany. But in other circumstances it might be a very difficult problem indeed. Again, if he believes that there are certain circumstances in which war is the least evil of the possible alternatives, and that it would be wrong to refuse to fight once these have arisen, it is all the more incumbent on him to look for ways of securing beforehand that such circumstances do not arise. But he would maintain that he would be fatally handicapped in his search for these if he laid it down beforehand that in no circumstances, however much they might be outside his own control, would he resort to war. Finally, he has to consider, much more fully than has been possible here, what attitude he wishes the society to which he belongs to adopt towards those who still remain Pacifist. On all these points it is clearly desirable that a settled public opinion should be formed, and to the formation of such an opinion clear thinking and rational argument will make their contribution. This book can claim no more than that it is an attempt to make such a contribution to the discussion of one of the many questions which arise in this connection, one which calls for a solution before the others can be faced.

INDEX

CAMBRIDGE: PRINTED BY W. LEWIS, M.A., AT THE UNIVERSITY PRESS